THE PURSUIT OF
HAPPINESS
AT WORK

For Entrepreneurs,
and the People Who
Work for Them

DOUG HICKOK

BLUE POOL MEDIA
ANNAPOLIS, MD

The Pursuit of Happiness at Work
For Entrepreneurs and the People Who Work for Them
Copyright © 2016 by Doug Hickok
All rights reserved.

The examples presented throughout the book are based on the author's experiences and those of the author's clients and others. Names, occupations, places, and other identifying details have been changed for reasons of confidentiality. In some cases, situations have been combined or modified to illustrate relevant points.

Cover design and interior layout by Julie Lundy (www.juliekaren.com)
Cover graphic by Freepik

Blue Pool Media
ISBN: 978-0-9862347-5-0
Printed in the United States of America

Dedicated to my wife,

BETSY HICKOK

and

THE BREAKFAST BUNCH

For your love, encouragement, and enthusiasm.

TABLE OF CONTENTS

INTRODUCTION

WHY HAPPINESS AT WORK MATTERS

When I first began to hear about the importance of workplace happiness, I also started getting a lot of feedback about the idea from my business-owner consulting clients. Most of it added up to this: "I want my people to be satisfied enough to do the work, but *happy* happy? If they get too happy, they'll never get anything done!"

So I did what I do and started digging into it. Exactly how do you make workers happy, and for that matter, what *is* happiness, exactly? Is there any research that can define what "workplace happiness" is, how it works, and what the real benefits are?

Yes, there is.

I went on to read a lot of research, and absolutely none of it said, "It's a fad" or "It doesn't work." I was struck by the fact that every summary of research I read, developed by serious people from around the world, said that happiness at work contributes to tangible, good outcomes, no matter what type or size of organization is involved.

When people are happy at work, they do their best work, they get along well with each other, and they stick with your company, all of which adds up to increased productivity and profits.

Happiness works at work.

Workers today are already advocating for a different, more human experience of work. The old grind-it-out-whether-or-not-you-enjoy-it workplaces are not the way of the future.

What we require to answer this need is a template for a happy workplace—some dance steps marked on the floor so we know how to get there.

In this book, you will find out:

- What happiness really is and how to create more of it
- The eight most important things workers need to be happy at work
- How to engage with young workers who have different work values so they will be productive and happy, and stay with your company
- What entrepreneurs need to do to strengthen and maintain their own happiness

Entrepreneurs are in a unique and wonderful position to improve the happiness of their workers. Even when they have large companies, entrepreneurs are all about agility and being able to change things fast—they thrive on change. That means they can take action to add the ingredients for workforce happiness into their workplaces quickly and effectively.

We do just about everything in life better when we are happy, and work is no exception. Our best work flows out of us when we feel happy; it's a no-brainer when you look at it that way.

So read on and get a twinkle in your eye, a spring in your step, and a renewed enthusiasm for your work. Happiness is good for you, it's good for your people, and it's definitely good for your bottom line.

PART 1
The Need for Happiness

CHAPTER 1

HAPPINESS AT WORK FOR YOU AND YOUR PEOPLE

Are your people happy to work for you?

Are you a happy business owner when you are at work?

The answers to these questions are more important than you may realize.

To enjoy your work and your workplace is a wonderful thing, but many people do not enjoy theirs, and it turns out that this is a very big business issue on a number of fronts. Most immediately, to grind through day after day of work that has little pleasure degrades body, mind, soul, and performance.

We are meant to bring joy and enthusiasm to daily living, to be attuned to our purpose—what we are really here on the planet to do—and to express that as much as possible in our lives. When we are on this track, we experience a deep sense of well-being, along with happy feelings ranging from satisfaction to delight.

When joy and aliveness don't show up with us at work, life loses its color and its juice in a very important way. We spend a lot of time where we'd rather not be, doing things we don't really want to do, and that goes against our human nature.

When we are unhappy at work, that absence of happiness radiates from us into our workplace. Our emotional state broadcasts itself out to everyone and sets the tone for how others interact with us. Unhappy people are seeds of more workforce unhappiness wherever they are because they seek connection with people who can share their emotional language.

We like to celebrate together, and we like to complain together.

In many companies, you've got your happy people paddling your "business boat" forward and your unhappy people paddling it backward. Visualize that for a moment—your business veering here and there with lots of paddling going on but not enough *forward* movement.

You may even be one of your unhappy people, and if you're a singer in that band, yours is the loudest voice, you have the biggest influence, and nobody else in your workplace will feel as though they have permission to be happy while you're singing the unhappiness song.

That's why this book isn't just about how to make your people happy. It is about that, but it is first about how to make *you* happy. You are the tuning fork that sets the tone for everyone in your organization, and your company needs you to be happy so your people can be happy. One drop of oil turns a clear glass of water dark, and if you are that dark drop in your business, any efforts you make to increase the happiness of your workers without first doing what you can to address your own happiness level will only do half the job.

How do we know this is true?

In my last book, *How to Succeed with Your Great Business Idea,* I talked about how important it is to approach your business *inside/ out*—how a business owner's desire to take action must be blended with inner thinking, imagining, guidance, planning, emotion, and intuition.

The power of this book is based upon a principle, too. It starts with you, the business owner, and it's about the principle of *emotional contagion.* People can "catch" each other's emotions like a virus when they work together. It doesn't matter what kind of emotions they are, happy or unhappy—we can catch them and pass them on.

We know, for instance, that what you as a leader think, feel, and do influences everyone around you. When the boss has a dark mood or a bad day, everyone senses that, hunkers down, and can catch that mood. Conversely, if the boss is happy, that feeling spreads through the ranks, too, and people loosen up and relax.

They do much better work when they are happy and relaxed, and so do you.

Another way we see this at work is to notice the big effect a couple of negative people can have on their work groups and, even more widely, on their entire organizations. We've all experienced how one unhappy person in an otherwise upbeat department or group can be that drop of toxic oil that darkens the emotional waters for everyone.

This is why your workplace can't really be a happy one without you—because your unhappiness will become their unhappiness through contagion. The good news is that it works the other way, too. If you are happy, then that is the emotion that spreads. That, along with other concrete actions you can take to increase the happiness and well-being of your people, will create a healthy, happy, and more profitable workplace.

But this thing of becoming a happy boss isn't always easy.

Many entrepreneurs see their own happiness at work as something optional—something that is dependent on their business becoming successful, often in specific ways. They'll be happy when revenues exceed five million dollars, or when they reach a certain market share percentage, or when the business is sold for a high price and they retire.

This is often the way business owners justify being miserable at work right now—by believing that their current unhappiness is a worthy sacrifice that will be redeemed later for a happy life.

The habit of being unhappy over time, even for a worthy result, is still a bad habit, and many entrepreneurs find, to their great chagrin, that they can't turn off their habitual unhappiness even when they reach their goals. It is set by that point and has become a way of life.

And, over all this time, emotional contagion is always influencing the happiness level of their workforce.

When you're in your office, what emotions do you, the leader, express every day? Your workers are, in many ways, absorbing and reflecting them and adapting to you.

Anyone who has kids knows how this works. Kids watch what their parents do and fall right in with that behavior. They live in your emotional environment and take it on themselves.

Your workers do the same thing.

Unhappy leaders don't have happy workers, and unhappy workers don't do great work.

Successful businesses, on the other hand, are very much about the journey as well as the outcomes. Their leaders know that the quality of the *daily work experience* for all their people is a key factor in creating great outcomes.

The most successful companies usually have a lot of happy people. Think United Healthcare, Amgen, Novartis International AG, and Nokia Corporation.

The measurable benefits of an organization having a happy leader and happy workers are substantial.

Authentic Happiness, a book by psychologist Martin Seligman, reports on the positive emotions of 272 company employees as part of a job performance study over an eighteen-month period. He concludes that happy people earn higher pay and better performance reviews.

D. G. Myers, in his book *The Pursuit of Happiness,* says his research shows that happy employees have lower medical costs and less absenteeism, and they work more efficiently.

A study by Case Western Reserve University reports that companies with happy people can save big through lower staff absences, talent retention, and productivity.

And another research project, conducted by the health insurance company Humana with the Ross School of Business at the University of Michigan, also strongly supports the economic value of workplace happiness.

In a six-year study of thirty-three nursing teams, the patients who worked with Humana's happiest, most engaged nurses had:

- 40% less paid out in claims
- 70% fewer visits to the ER for their patients
- 91% fewer patient visits to urgent care clinics

This reduced Humana's service delivery costs for the happy nurses' patients by 24%!

Research from these and other sources shows that happy workers:

- Are more productive
- Work better with others
- Are more creative
- Are more innovative
- Are more solution-oriented
- Focus more on what is right than what is wrong

- Stay at their jobs longer
- Make better decisions
- Are better leaders
- Are more open and less defensive
- Are less inclined toward conflict
- Have more energy
- Are more optimistic
- Are more motivated
- Have fewer absences
- Worry less
- Learn faster

All these advantages contribute significantly to a company's profitability and long-term success.

CHAPTER 2

HAPPY COMPANIES FIND AND KEEP SKILLED WORKERS

Predictions are dire about where American business is heading when it comes to attracting, hiring, and retaining the workers it needs.

It seems that the supply of skilled workers is falling behind demand, and worker happiness is now being seen as a competitive advantage to recruit and retain the right people in a more competitive labor market.

Happy companies have always had a recruiting advantage, but many of those companies have been small or midsized entrepreneurial organizations, and how they create more happiness in their workplaces has not been of interest to bigger enterprises until recently. The word is out, though, and companies of every size are scrambling onto the happiness-at-work bandwagon. Here's why.

According to the US Department of Labor, the United States has a skilled labor shortage for which there is no end in sight, at least until workplace automation swallows up enough human jobs twenty or thirty years down the road to reduce the number of workers needed in the workforce and close the gap. For now, the number of available skilled workers is decreasing, while our total population is steadily increasing, so more people require more goods and services at a time when the number of skilled workers is not keeping up with the demand.

The problem is compounded because it is getting harder and harder for companies to find and hire these workers, even during economic downturns. There always used to be a large pool of skilled workers available during a recession because of a high general level of unemployment. That has changed—skilled workers and knowledge workers (those for whom the product of their thinking is a major part of their job) are hard to find and are being hired quickly in any economy.

Those workers are the new rock stars in this emerging recruiting shortage. The competition for their services is fierce, and giving them the option to be in a happy workplace has a huge influence on how they make their employment choices.

This incoming workforce of new, young workers is different from the generations that came before because they don't feel much loyalty to a company. They see how coldly companies have historically treated their workers, so they increasingly view work as a means to an end to achieve more important personal goals. One of their biggest goals is to be happy and enjoy life, and if a job doesn't provide an environment for that, they won't work there if they have a choice. Or, they will work there until they can hop on over to a happier workplace.

Equipped with a smartphone, today's unhappy worker who gets fed up in the morning can find a new job on his lunch break. Through social media platforms, workers also know which organizations are good to work for and which ones are not. They know which companies demand total loyalty to the god of work and which companies will give you room for a good life while you do your good work.

When I do executive coaching with employers and we talk about this shift in worker priorities, some of those business owners get a sour look on their faces and blame these new-breed workers for having no sense of responsibility, no drive, and no loyalty. They see them as deficient and lazy, and they don't know how to deal with them.

This clash of value systems and viewpoints has actually been brewing for some time now.

The traditional core message of business to workers for a long time has been something like this: *If you work really hard and invest your time and effort in your work, it will give you a good life.*

Today's young job candidates hear that but don't believe it, because as children they watched their parents buy into that promise and be consumed by their work. So their message for employers is, *I will not live to work—I will work to live.*

Into that simmering tension comes the Department of Labor report about the shortage of skilled workers—about how hard it is to find them and keep them.

That report is a gun to the head of all employers, and they know it.

Regardless of their deeply held traditional values about how work and workers should be, employers are coming to realize that they must find common ground with this new breed of worker or their companies will not thrive, or even survive. Many of them are now trying to understand and meet the reordered needs of their job applicants. They are experimenting with how to provide a work environment that supports a happy experience for those employees at work, and they are also trying to come up with work policies that allow employees to have a good life away from work.

Happiness in the workplace matters now. Yes indeed, it does. Times. Have. Changed.

So now we have all these companies trying to find an edge in the escalating recruiting and retention wars, and they rightly know that a happy workplace is a big asset in the new world of work. American businesses are experimenting with all kinds of offerings to develop more happiness—whatever that might look like—for their people.

They have tried various new perks and cool benefits in the workplace, some of which contribute to worker happiness, and some of which don't. They have offered gourmet cafeterias, workout gyms, and bringing your dog to work with mixed results. The bottom line on happiness incentives seems to be that you can't just throw more perks at people and expect their real level of happiness to change for the better. It's not that simple.

This new owner/worker relationship that is being forged through a combination of high job performance, a high quality of life at work, and real support for a good life outside of work is complex and requires real changes. Attitudes, policies, cultures, and actions all the way up and down in organizations need adjustment before those organizations become preferred employers for the new workers they will need.

This is true whether you have a small business or a large one.

CHAPTER 3
WHAT IS HAPPINESS, ANYWAY?

We've got this pursuit-of-happiness thing all wrong, you know.

Our Declaration of Independence says Americans have an "inalienable right" to pursue happiness. The pursuit of happiness was considered to be so important to our country's founders that they enshrined it in our constitution, right up there in the beginning of the document, on a level with life and liberty.

So how has that been working out for us—how has the happiness search been going?

In today's America, we don't really understand very well how happiness works—what it takes in practical terms to be happy. Our digital devices tell us we can be happy right now by pushing this button or buying that thing. Instant gratification rules, but that is not the real deal about happiness; it's just the stimulation of some happy buzz.

The right to pursue happiness as stated in the Declaration of Independence is usually interpreted today as the right to go after whatever would make us *feel* happy, but that is not what the Framers of the document meant by happiness.

So, if happiness isn't what we thought it was, what is it? Let's start with a working definition of the word.

The dictionary makes a mess of it:

"The state of being happy. Pleasure, contentment, satisfaction, cheerfulness, merriment, gaiety, joy, joyfulness, joviality, jollity, glee, delight, good spirits, lightheartedness, well-being, enjoyment, exuberance, exhilaration, elation, ecstasy, jubilation, rapture, bliss, blissfulness, euphoria, transports of delight, Hollywood ending."

"Hollywood ending," for Pete's sake?

Here is another definition, from Princeton's *WordNet*, that comes closer to the Founders' definition: "Happiness is a state of well-being characterized by emotions ranging from contentment to intense joy."

"A state of well-being" sounds as though it would include much more than momentary good feelings, doesn't it? "A state of well-being" suggests being *located* in well-being, not just passing through it. And, this deeper state of well-being stimulates happy feelings that range from contentment to intense joy.

Well-being and feelings of happiness are thus related, but they are not the same thing.

A "state of well-being" is closer to the Founders' definition of happiness as it was understood in their time. The Framers of the Declaration defined the well-being parts of happiness to include personal prosperity—one's physical and emotional needs should be met—but they believed that happiness had moral and spiritual elements as well. Happiness wasn't just about meeting your own needs; you also needed to be moral and spiritual out in the world and take part in community life.

That was the Founders' recipe for happiness.

In recent times, US Supreme Court Justice Anthony Kennedy was greatly concerned about our latter-day misunderstanding of the constitutional meaning of happiness. He wrote,

> "In this era, happiness carries with it the connotation of self-pleasure; there is a hedonistic component to the definition now. However, that's not what Jefferson meant, and it's not what the Framers meant.

> "If you read (George) Washington, he uses the term happiness all the time, as did the other members of the generation at the time of the founding. For them, happiness meant that feeling of self-worth and dignity you acquire by contributing to your community and its civic life."

Justice Kennedy is saying that a state of well-being—in this case, derived from contributions made to community and civic life—brought about a perception of self-worth and dignity in the Declaration Framers that made them feel happy.

This part of the Declaration might have been clearer if it had been stated as, "We hold these truths to be self-evident, that all men are created equal, that they are endowed by their Creator with certain Inalienable Rights, that among these are Life, Liberty, and the *pursuit of well-being*."

There were, in fact, various communications between the Founders about their concern that the word *happiness* could be misinterpreted, just as it has been, but it ended up in the Declaration anyway.

There is also an important misunderstanding about the "pursuit" of happiness that needs to be cleared up, while we're at it.

The Framers' use of the word *pursuit,* as in "the pursuit of happiness," has also been widely misunderstood in our time to mean the act of searching for, or looking for, happiness. In the Founders' time, the English language was used differently, and *pursuit* was more commonly used in a here-and-now way, such as, "He is in pursuit of a career in law." In the meaning of the times, this wording would mean that he is *currently practicing law*. He's not looking for an opportunity to practice law in the future, he's not searching for it—he's actively engaging in it now. It is this meaning of the word *pursuit* that was intended in the Declaration phrase.

Our interpretation of the word *pursuit* in the Declaration as being about finding something as yet unknown has caused us to wrongly think that happiness is some mysterious quality of life that is hard to find and must be sought after rather than something that can be known and achieved in the present with the right focus and attention.

So, in the time of the Declaration, "the pursuit of happiness" wasn't just about looking for ways to feel happy emotions. It was about finding and living in a state of well-being in the present that would bring with it feelings of happiness ranging from contentment to intense joy.

This is a much deeper, richer definition of "the pursuit of happiness" than we have believed it to be, and a more complex view of what it takes to achieve happiness than just thinking of it as a set of feelings to be sought and experienced.

Happy feelings are real and desirable, and the situations in which we feel them vary greatly, but at their core is a sense of well-being, no matter how brief, from which those feelings come in every such circumstance. Well-being is the foundation for happiness that the Founders wanted us to put together and live from.

What does this mean for today's workers if you're trying to make them happier?

It means that you can't just trot out stuff for your employees that will make them smile. You must go deeper than that and create an environment at work that will add to their fundamental sense of well-being. When you do that, they will be happy, which will then be a big gain for your well-being and happiness as a business owner, too.

Since *feeling* happy in a long-lasting way depends upon having the foundation of an internal state of well-being, let's look at how you might build that foundation for yourself and for your people at work. Once you know how to do that, you can certainly create meaningful happiness throughout your workplace and wherever else you might want it.

The dictionary once again comes up short in its effort to define well-being:

"The state of being comfortable, healthy, or happy."

Nope. They might as well have put question marks after the words *comfortable, healthy,* and *happy* because you can feel that they're just guessing and throwing words together.

A feeling of happiness can be brief or long-lasting, deep or shallow. A bird's song, a found ten-dollar bill, a brilliant sunrise—each moves us to feel good and can make us feel momentarily happy. Life is full of such wonderful short-term blooms of happiness, and they are important and add to our underlying sense of well-being. But for happiness that connects all the parts of our lives—including work—and that endures over time, the state of well-being that supports it must also be long-term.

An example: Let's say you have work you really like and a family that is loving and supportive, and you feel that you're moving toward a future that you desire. You are a fair and respectful person, and you find ways to give back to your community and the world. These elements of your life, all coming together to form a deep and wide sense of well-being, would tend to bring lots of feelings of happiness with them. If your underlying sense of well-being stays strong over time, you would probably even identify those happy feelings as a context for your life, as in, *I am a happy woman or man.*

This does not mean that a state of well-being generates happy feelings all the time or that you don't get to have the sometimes-serious problems that come with being alive. What it means is that your pains and sorrows exist within an overall context of ongoing happiness and that there is room for the trials of life as part of your happiness. When your foundation of well-being is strong, it supports you through ups and downs.

Happy feelings arise from a state of well-being the way smoke rises from a fire, and those feelings vary for each of us. For some people, the emotions of happiness are big, celebratory, and loud, but for others they might be quiet, hidden, and deep.

Here are forty happiness-related emotions:

Alive	*Content*	*Cheerful*	*Delighted*
Elated	*Excited*	*Exhilarated*	*Exuberant*
Fearless	*Gleeful*	*Joyful*	*Overjoyed*
Satisfied	*Tender*	*Loving*	*Passionate*
Close	*Eager*	*Inspired*	*Determined*
Enthusiastic	*Optimistic*	*Confident*	*Hopeful*
Free	*Secure*	*Playful*	*Energetic*
Liberated	*Thrilled*	*Calm*	*Peaceful*
Comfortable	*Encouraged*	*Relaxed*	*Eager*
Happy	*Glad*	*Jubilant*	*Serene*
Receptive	*Boisterous*		

CHAPTER 4

THE SEVENTY PERCENT

Two million two hundred forty thousand people Google the word *happy* every month, so a whole lot of pursuing of happiness is still going on. We look for happiness on Google, in our romantic relationships, in our families, and at work, although the work part isn't going so well right now.

Until recent times, happiness was only thought to be possible or even desirable in one's personal life. Work was work, and whether or not you were happy about it wasn't that important. "It's work—you're not supposed to be happy!" was what your father or your boss would likely say if you whined about being unhappy at work.

Some people have been fortunate to love their work anyway and to enjoy it immensely, or to work in one of the minority of businesses that truly value and foster happiness as being essential to work. Many more, though, have not had that experience.

A Gallup *State of the American Workplace* study found that 70% of those who participated described themselves as disengaged from their work, and only 30% of the 150,000 people surveyed said they enjoy their jobs. The biggest single reason given for disengagement and unhappiness at work was "the boss." Gallup CEO Jim Clifton says, "Managers from hell are creating active disengagement costing the United States an estimated $450 billion to $550 billion annually."

There are indeed many supervisors, managers, and business owners who aren't very good at being the boss, but there is a lot more to the lack of engagement in business today than that. Bosses are just a product of the system that made them bosses, and the system is not about happiness—it's mostly about profits.

That system has been the real problem, expressed as it is through its people.

If we were to imagine what a state of well-being would look like that would be central to the happiness of businesses, we would find that it has historically been about the various aspects of profit accumulation. It has not included happiness or other personal concerns as necessary ingredients for business success—just those human factors and attributes that directly and observably influence profits.

Are there good people in business who care about their people, too? Yes, but it is also acceptable as a business principle to make decisions that give heavier weight to profitability than people. I don't mean by this that profits aren't important—they are. And there are successful businesses that find a way to give equal weight to profits and people, which is a lot of what workers are asking for from businesses these days—a more "profits *and* people" set of priorities and state of mind.

But, these changes are hard for businesses to make because they have a cultural history to overcome.

One of the biggest early factors in the evolution of the American workplace was the Puritan work ethic. The religious group that came over on the *Mayflower* and settled northeastern America was composed of Puritans, whom we more commonly refer to as the Pilgrims.

One of their strongest beliefs—the one that really took hold in the American work ethos—was that hard work creates all good things. Hard work, mind you, not happy work. Workplace happiness was not even a concept then, and they also believed that idleness was a sin.

So for the Puritans, work was a very consuming, serious, hard thing, but you needed to do it, and if you didn't, something was wrong with you.

Sound familiar?

Sixty-hour weeks, no vacations, email all the time, and your business mind turned on 24/7? Put your feelings aside at work so you can be "all business?" It's the modern version of the Puritan work ethic.

That's what American business has been about until now, hasn't it?

This belief that hard work makes everything happen was a great fit with the America of early times, when just about everything that had to be done to survive and get ahead inherently did involve a lot of hard work. The Industrial Revolution hadn't happened back then, and you wrestled the earth behind a mule to plant crops. You cut down trees manually to build a house by hand and performed many other acts necessary for survival directly through the energy of your human body. Hard work was utterly necessary every day, and the belief that hard work was of great value was a natural and sensible one for the time.

Not so for happiness.

It was possible in Puritan times to have property, money, and a certain type of Godly joy, but happiness for its own sake, just to be happy, was not part of the picture. Joy at work was not seen as desirable, except for the joy of doing hard work as a gift to God and the community.

The Puritan work ethic, also known as the Protestant work ethic, survived as the backbone of the American work ethic until very recently, and this is where American business is coming from as it tries to grapple with the need for happiness in the workplace in these very different times. Workers were—and still are, to some extent—supposed to suck it up, leave their personal needs and lives outside the workplace door, and be serious and focused only on (hard) work.

Think about that. The Puritan work ethic was so demanding that it called for us to carve ourselves in two, one part for who we really are (outside of work) and another part for what we do (at work).

Any psychologist will tell you that splitting oneself like that has undesirable consequences, and that's putting it mildly.

There is still a need for hard work in business, of course, but it is a very big deal that happiness, a very personal state of being, is now becoming a work value, too. It is a giant, difficult step to take for the business world, given its impersonal, grind-it-out history.

So, what is the American work ethic now if it isn't all about hard work?

A lot of people would say it is "work smarter, not harder." This widely used phrase questions the old dependence on hard work as the primary way to get things done. It makes the statement that reducing hard work by thinking of better, more efficient alternatives is good.

That right there is a work ethic revolution.

And what is behind the revolution? Why do workers now want so much more than hard work and a paycheck?

PART 2
The Happiness Revolution

CHAPTER 5

THE EVOLUTION OF WHAT WE WANT

Psychologist Abraham Maslow developed his theory of human motivation, otherwise known as Maslow's Hierarchy of Needs, in 1943. This hierarchy has stood the test of time and is illustrated in the pyramid below. To understand it, we begin at the bottom and read up:

SELF-ACTUALIZATION

Morality, creativity, spontaneity,
acceptance, purpose, meaning,
and inner potential

SELF-ESTEEM

Confidence, achievement, respect of others,
self-respect, the need to be a unique individual

LOVE AND BELONGING

Family, friendship, community, a sense of connection

SAFETY AND SECURITY

Out of danger—stability, structure, order—health, employment

PHYSIOLOGICAL NEEDS

Body needs: food, water, shelter, clothing, activity, sleep, sex

As you can see, we develop as human beings from our physical survival needs up through a number of other types of needs to reach a robust sense of self-understanding and fulfillment. Each level of development depends on having sufficient achievement of the ones below it to provide a foundation for advancement.

Maslow's levels are usually associated with internal personal development. As people grow inside, however, they want work and life to grow with them, so I am using Maslow's levels as a way to show how people's personal development is connected to the evolution of their desires and expectations in the workplace.

Back before the Industrial Revolution, life was agrarian—farm and family based—and small businesses providing food, tools, and other necessities operated out of peoples' homes. There were no big businesses as we know them now, and people didn't have a lot of choice about where they lived or what they did for a living.

Much of life in those days was heavily focused on Maslow's level one—physical needs and survival. People might have had a taste of higher levels here and there, but life was generally short and not so sweet.

Then the Industrial Revolution came from Great Britain to America and completely transformed our continent from about 1760 to the early 1800s.

This intense period of the invention of new machinery and manufacturing processes changed work forever. People moved from farms to cities, companies were formed, workers were hired, and the industrial age was off to a roaring start. The development of time—and energy—saving technologies allowed workers to start moving up through Maslow's Hierarchy of Needs into having less constricted values and desires, and it also brought about a great deal more personal and work mobility.

Initially, wealth was highly concentrated among the owners of railroads, shipping companies, and manufacturing facilities. There were only owners' rules in the new workplaces—kids working fifteen hours a day alongside adults with no time off—so workers initially were still mired in Maslow's level one of barely getting by and trying to stay alive.

The 1800s that followed were a constant battle between workers and business owners to set some rules for work. Labor uprisings, unions, and court settlements ultimately produced laws and policies that made work life more bearable for workers, and as time went by they began to experience more of Maslow's level two, where they had some safety, stability, and connection in their lives.

Fast-forward to 1920 and the birth of the electronic age, when the introduction of broadcast radio was a gigantic step forward in the happiness revolution.

No matter where people were, they could hear about faraway events in real time, and the whole world of other people, places, and things came right into their living rooms. They were no longer limited in their awareness of the world to their family, their town, or their job.

The first commercial television station came on the air in America in 1928, and it wasn't long before we could also see the rest of the world as well as hear it.

What people saw and heard on those broadcasts sometimes made them want to pick up and move, and a lot of people did. Radio and television sparked an unprecedented wave of worker mobility as people moved to change their lives and change their jobs. They wanted what they heard about on their radios and saw on their televisions.

World War II led to widespread business prosperity in America through the creation of a large number of companies and jobs to fulfill war needs. Businesses prospered after the war, innovation was rapid in every industry, and workers became more skillful and knowledgeable about their work and their job choices.

For forty years following the war, workers were upward bound and on the move, solidifying their work roles and incomes to achieve Maslow's levels two and three:

Level 2: Out of danger—stability, structure, order, health, and employment

Level 3: Love and belonging—family, friendship, community, intimacy, and a sense of connection

Material prosperity was increasing all the time, and the marketplace was filled with lots of new things to buy with those bigger paychecks. Life was pretty good—America's businesses and workers had come a long way.

CHAPTER 6

COMPANIES AND WORKERS: THE GREAT DIVIDE GETS WIDER

Even during this postwar period of great prosperity, the seeds of a more adversarial relationship between companies and their workers were being planted.

On the company side, organizations learned how to be much more efficient in their operations, which reduced the numbers of workers they needed to hire. Layoffs, at first rare and only used in response to urgent financial or production problems, became more widespread as a routine way of adjusting to markets and managing costs. New technologies and business efficiencies made it possible to squeeze more work from the fewer employees who were left, and machines gradually took over many jobs previously held by people.

This evolution of the workplace caused employers to have less loyalty to their workers, and workers to have less loyalty to their employers, so the long-standing and more personal owner/worker compact that had been a binding force between company owners and workers for a long time began to erode.

Both sides became more strategic and calculating, and less trusting, in their dealings with each other.

The older compact, within which workers were more likely to stay at a job for a long time and contribute more directly to the core operations of a company, involved an unspoken reciprocal understanding between owners and labor that went something like this: "We're all in this together, we need each other, and we'll take care of each other."

When machines started replacing people and workers moved from job to job more often, "We're in this together" became, "I'm in this for myself" all the way around, and that changed the nature of work in America—it polarized business owners and workers, and business relationships became more *transaction-based* instead of *relationship-based*. Workers and companies started looking out for their own interests without the former reciprocal concern for each other, so it came to be that not many workers and companies looked out for each other anymore.

When transactions replace relationships—when what you do for me is more important than what we do for each other—loyalty to each other disappears, and behaviors emerge on both sides that are uncaring and self-serving. This reduces happiness and trust for everyone, and it gets in the way of collaborations and functions necessary for doing the work itself.

Into this estrangement came the 1980s digital revolution, which kicked any remaining business/worker loyalties into the ditch by the side of the road.

The pace at which machines replaced human functions at work accelerated and continues to accelerate to this day.

The introduction and widespread use of personal computers in the home, followed by the progression of sophisticated portable devices that are now with us everywhere, eliminated lag time in life and at work. Letters take days to arrive; an email takes a second. Telephones used to be a fast way to communicate, but now we have full video and voice communication anywhere, anytime.

Digital technologies spreading through the business world caused waves of restructurings and employee reductions even as specialized new jobs were created by rapidly advancing technologies. The demand for skilled and knowledge workers grew fast, and the demand for unskilled labor went into continual decline.

Change, in both life and the workplace, before the advent of the Internet tended to be sequential—this thing happened and then that thing happened—but it is exponential now. Change happens at an ever-increasing speed with no end to its acceleration in sight.

This wind tunnel of turbulent, constant workplace change and the toxic "it's all about my needs" transactional nature of many business/worker relationships today are the biggest factors that have produced that stunning 70% rate of disengagement from their jobs by American workers.

Workers don't feel valued or secure in their jobs in the transactional work environment, and they also don't feel secure because of automation and the constant squeeze for more and more production in their jobs. This prevents them from having a solid sense of well-being, which is a necessary foundation for happiness.

Supervisors and other bosses are the faces of the transactional business model in action. They are tangible targets for worker anger because bosses implement the transactional ethic in their interactions with their workers every day. That's why they are cited by workers in the Gallup survey as the reason for so much worker disengagement.

All this is enough to make one queasy, cross-eyed, and cranky, but it is also the backdrop for a new and hopeful conversation about the need to connect work with personal happiness. There is a great need for happiness repair in today's workplace because so many people are feeling quite low when it comes to their well-being.

So you see, even if you are an entrepreneur who tries hard to run a business with good people values and practices, your workers often come to you with a job history that has been quite different, and they bring issues with them that can keep them from aligning well with you. They are often unhappy, tired, and numb from the damage done by bad bosses and an uncaring work ethic.

It will take your own happiness and caring, plus good leadership and a real plan, to repair the damage that has been done to your workers by this "new economy."

PART 3
The Happy Entrepreneur

CHAPTER 7

THE BIGGEST REASONS PEOPLE BECOME ENTREPRENEURS

*"Often people attempt to live their lives backwards;
they try to have more things or more money in order
to do more of what they want so they will be happier.
The way it actually works is the reverse. You must
first be who you really are, then do what you need to
do in order to have what you want."*
—Margaret Young

I wrote earlier that you must be a happy leader for your workers to be happy, but it's a little more complicated than that.

Perhaps you're not happy for good reasons that you can't change right now. It might be because of your health, a family situation, or other troubles of almost any kind. Genetics may also be involved. Some people and their families are to happiness as antimatter is to matter—they just can't go there.

Even if you *are* happy, your face and manner might not show it. I'm one of those people whose mouth tends to turn down at the corners when I'm not talking, and this can be misinterpreted as unhappiness.

So you are probably not going to radiate high levels of happiness if these factors are in play. Does this mean your people are doomed to be unhappy because you're not happy? No, but you'll have to work a little harder to create an environment where they can feel good even when you don't.

More about that shortly, but first let's take a look at what makes entrepreneurs happy. Most entrepreneurs become business owners for one or more of the following reasons:

1. ENTREPRENEURS ARE PURSUING A PASSION, DOING WHAT THEY LOVE, AND FULFILLING A DREAM.

When one of my business-owner clients told me about an employee who had a cake-baking business on the side, I advised her to be prepared for that person to quit at some point to launch her baking venture as a full-time business because that was where her passion was. Sure enough, six months later she was gone.

2. ENTREPRENEURS HAVE FINANCIAL AND LIFE-STYLE GOALS THEY WANT TO ACHIEVE THAT WON'T HAPPEN IN A JOB.

Being employed in a job limits advancement, pay, and free time. Personal and professional goals that are bigger than those limits beg to be realized in some other way.

3. ENTREPRENEURS WANT UNLIMITED POTENTIAL.

For entrepreneurs, there are potentially no limits on income or lifestyle, and they can be themselves at work. Nobody is telling them what they can't do or how much money they can't make.

4. ENTREPRENEURS KNOW THEY AREN'T CUT OUT TO WORK FOR OTHER PEOPLE.

Some people who should be working for themselves instead of someone else know that right off the bat, but others don't realize it until they have many frustrating experiences holding down a job.

5. ENTREPRENEURS HAVE A DESIRE FOR FREEDOM AND AUTONOMY.

The chained dog barks, and the entrepreneur whose working hours, routines, and methods are laid out for him or her by someone else is an unhappy beast indeed. Freedom beckons, and he or she either finds a way out or burns out.

6. ENTREPRENEURS NEED TO BE IN CONTROL— TO BE IN CHARGE OF WHAT'S HAPPENING.

Entrepreneurs are wired to be in charge because they know they can do better than the boss. They won't be happy until they get their chance to prove it.

7. ENTREPRENEURS HAVE HAD IT WITH THE DAILY FRUSTRATIONS AND LIMITATIONS OF EMPLOYMENT.

They usually have a long frustration list—bad bosses, toxic workplaces, no room to grow, too many work hours and not enough time off, having to say yes when they mean no. Yep, it's a long list.

8. ENTREPRENEURS WANT TO GET OUT OF THE RAT RACE.

There are roughly twice as many people in the world now as there were in 1970, and entrepreneurs-at-heart who haven't left their jobs yet ride sardine-like with the mob on the commuter trains every day. Sooner or later, though, they find the courage to flee from the endless commute to and from their stressful jobs that pay the bills but aren't much fun.

9. ENTREPRENEURS WANT TO MAKE A POSITIVE DIFFERENCE IN THE WORLD.

Sometimes the public perception of people in business is that they are greedy and self-serving. This negative stereotype does exist—there are businesspeople like that—but most entrepreneurs want to have a positive impact and change the world in some way for the better while they achieve their financial and life goals.

And there you have it—nine of the biggest motivations that attract people to entrepreneurship.

You should keep whichever ones that are yours alive in your mind and emblazoned upon your heart. You need a strong "why" to keep something as complex and challenging as a business going over time.

And, there is more to your choice of entrepreneurship than these reasons.

Researchers say that 50% of our individual happiness comes from our history, genetics, personality, family, and environment, and the other 50% is up to us.

This means that the degree to which you have been able to successfully fulfill your reasons for wanting to be an entrepreneur, combined with what's going on with those other happiness factors that the researchers are talking about, determines how happy you are with your work right now.

Remember, I am talking about the authentic happiness that comes with well-being—feeling solid about where you are and where you are going in your life.

Ah, yes, your life.

It's really hard to have much happiness at work if the rest of your life is a mess. This book is primarily about happiness at work, but I would be remiss if I didn't hook that up with the fact that happiness doesn't observe work or life boundaries. It goes both ways; if you're miserable at work, you will probably be unhappy at home as well, and a poor home life cannot adequately support the happiness you find at work. Happiness is contagious, though, and as you have more of it, everything across all the borders of your life is influenced by it.

So, wouldn't it be nice if you could measure how happy you are at work, and then you could know exactly where you are happy and where you are not? You would be able to strengthen the happiness you have and make some choices about the unhappy places in order to improve them.

There are ways to do that.

CHAPTER 8
YOUR WORKPLACE HAPPINESS MAP

Some of the reasons I've listed for becoming an entrepreneur may have been yours, and some may not have fit your situation. Whatever the combination of reasons that moved you to start your own business, you went for it, and if you are like most entrepreneurs, the results have been somewhat of a mixed bag. You may be enjoying many of the benefits of business ownership that you hoped for, but each of those motivating reasons also has a downside and generally doesn't turn out to be as simple as you might have wished. It's true of life generally, isn't it, that the reality of anything important we do is usually more complicated than our ideas and hopes about it at the beginning? The meaningful choices we make in life become a lot more complex once we act upon them.

This is definitely true for entrepreneurs when it comes to the difference between the hopes and dreams that lead us into opening a business and the realities we face once we are actually running that business every day.

What comes next in this book is a look at some of the most common complications you're likely to run into for each of those *biggest reasons that people become entrepreneurs.* I spotlight challenges in each area that derail happiness for many entrepreneurs and offer solutions that can keep you on course if they apply to you.

I invite you to keep track of the items in this section that you think could be true about you and your business—things that might be getting in the way of your happiness. You can score your happiness for each item, see how you're doing, and also get some good recommendations for remedies.

If you take this section to heart and really work with it, this is how you, the leader of your company, can increase your happiness, which will then make it possible for you to increase the happiness of your people.

If, as you read along, you find that you are performing reasonably well across all the reasons behind your decision to become an entrepreneur, you are probably quite happy at work overall. Even so, there will likely be areas that could use a tweak here and there.

CHAPTER 9

HOW TO GET ORGANIZED AND WORK FROM YOUR STRENGTHS

For many entrepreneurs, being a business owner can turn into the worst job in the company because it is hard to have a well-organized approach to your business as

> **THE BIGGEST REASON PEOPLE BECOME ENTREPENEURS:**
>
> **ENTREPRENEURS ARE PURSUING A PASSION, DOING WHAT THEY LOVE, AND FULFILLING A DREAM.**

it grows. Every part of the company needs to support the growth of the company as a whole, and getting all those parts to synchronize is a very difficult thing. Sales may take off like a rocket, so you add more salespeople. This creates an immediate need for more people and infrastructure to support the increased sales in all the other areas of the company, from admin to customer service. One part of the business grows, and the others must adjust.

As needs multiply and the company grows, the need for your involvement everywhere seems to grow as well. As your enterprise gets bigger and more complex, you probably come in too early and stay too late, and you may feel chained to your desk with few opportunities to take time off.

Unless you define and carve out a detailed job description for yourself that is flexible enough to grow with your company, you can get sucked into this growth vortex headfirst and never come up for air. Increased demands on your time create impossible prioritization conflicts for you unless you have systems in place that will keep you focused on a core set of tasks that only *you* should really do at every stage of business development.

A train needs tracks to run on, and an excellent job description is the track that every person in your organization—beginning with you—needs to have in order to function well and move your company forward.

The function of a job description, at its core, is to turn the loose facts about the functional needs of a job into a complete and clear script for the position. Everything that needs to be done—and by whom—is outlined for action.

The lack of clear, detailed job descriptions is at the heart of great mischief and so many dysfunctions in a high percentage of companies that struggle. When there aren't good, clear job descriptions, there is no foundation for accountability; people don't have guidelines and limits for their work, and they stray hither and yon, making a fine mess along the way.

Here is an example from a company where I consulted about a variety of issues that all turned out to be connected:

Company "A" has been purchased by a new owner who installs her new president, Mark, to run it.

Mark has a contract and a plan, but he does not have a written job description.

President Mark forms an executive team of department heads to lead the company with him.

All the department heads have their original job descriptions, which have not been updated to reflect the changes brought about by the purchase of the company.

The former president of company "A," Jack, who sold the company, has been kept on board in a different role by the new owner. He is now the head of its product development department. Jack was the original product innovator and founder of company "A."

Former president Jack does not have a written job description, and his only charge by the new owner is to "develop good products."

By now, as you read this, you are no doubt twitching in your chair and figuratively or actually covering your eyes because you know a train wreck is coming.

President Mark's hands are more than full; his responsibilities are stacked as high as the sky as he works to steer company "A" through many changes. Everyone needs a piece of him all day long, and he's overwhelmed by the torrent. His leadership and task management become urgency-oriented—whoever has the loudest voice and the most urgent need gets his attention first. Quieter things that are important get lost.

Meanwhile, former president Jack roams the halls, ducking into offices and giving his opinions and advice to those who will listen. Since he was their president until very recently, people listen, and often what he says is in direct conflict with what current president Mark says, so supervisors and employees are whiplashed and paralyzed by the dual input.

Jack decides which meetings he will or will not attend, and he comes and goes unpredictably. Sometimes he doesn't show up for days on end, and nobody knows where he is.

Because he is rich from the proceeds of selling the business, and because he has a contract but no job description, Jack can draw outside the lines in all these destructive ways without any accountability for anything he does. He is essential to the company, but he has no incentives to follow any leader but his own desires.

Because president Mark has no job description, he's winging it most days instead of following his plan—doing his best to prioritize on the fly. His time management has gone out the window, and he's looking haggard.

Various departmental personnel changes have been made, but because department heads don't have updated job descriptions that reflect those changes, they are confused about who does what and where the accountability is now.

So company "A" is convulsed through its transition instead of moving through it with unified leadership, and the ongoing convulsion is influenced greatly by the fact that those leaders don't have the boundaries that good job descriptions impose. They don't know their limits, so they get all over each other, and conflict and confusion are the order of the day.

SCORING

Give yourself a score for how organized and structured you are about running your whole business, on a scale of 1 to 10. (1 is "I'm not organized very well, and it really gets in the way of my happiness," and 10 is "My organization is good, and I'm happy with how I'm doing in this area.")

Your score between 1 and 10 is _____.

THE FIX

You need a really good job description. Before you can have one, though, you must know: a) what you're really good at—your strengths—and b) which of those tasks you're currently doing that fully align with your strengths and are tasks that only you should be doing. Once you know those things, you will have the information you need to create a good job description for yourself, which will also serve as a written set of boundaries from which you should not stray.

Here's how you can get to know your strengths.

We all work better and are happier when we're doing what we do best. The Gallup organization, publishers of the Clifton Strengthsfinder assessment, defines strengths and talents this way: "A strength is the ability to consistently provide near-perfect performance in a specific activity. Talents are naturally recurring patterns of thought, feeling, or behavior that can be productively applied. Talents, knowledge, and skills—along with the time spent (i.e., investment) practicing, developing your skills, and building your knowledge base—combine to create your strengths."

So what you ideally want is an organization where everyone—you, most of all—is working from their strengths. In reality, way too many people are assigned to positions, projects, and tasks on the basis of their past experience and training, with no thought given to their actual strengths. Leaders assume and hope that applicants are strong in all the critical skills for their positions, but this is not always true.

I am reminded of a company where I was called in to assist in filling a CFO (Chief Financial Officer) position after their own hiring efforts fell short. It's a great company to work for and the pay is good, but the owner had already been through two bad hires for this position, both people having turned out to be very low in crucial strengths.

The first person they hired turned out to have impeccable accounting skills but was really poor in his interactions with people. This is a somewhat common profile for accounting professionals, but in this case his job description required him to supervise a twelve-person accounting office, so people skills were absolutely necessary.

The second hire had all the requisite accounting and people skills, but he was excessively detail oriented. Now, you'd think that a lot of detail orientation in an accountant is a good thing, but this guy was so down in the weeds with every little detail of everything department-wide that he never got around to delivering his own completed work in an adequate or timely way.

A lot of time and money were wasted because the hiring of these people did not include enough detailed information about their true strengths, nor was there any information about what strengths were undeveloped or lacking in them.

This is the first of two major ways that a failure to be strengths-oriented can damage your company.

The second way is to take people with a certain set of strengths and give them positions or tasks that are not oriented toward their strengths.

As I worked with one company to strengthen its sales force, for instance, the job description for the lead sales position required the candidate to be a top-level salesperson and to also be good at all the record keeping that is required to back up the sales. I knew that any salesperson who was hired with this dual requirement of being a salesperson and a record keeper would probably be very good at sales and really terrible at record keeping because those are two completely incompatible sets of strengths, and it is nearly impossible to find someone who is good at both of them. I advised the business owner to separate the record keeping from the sales function. Sure enough, he found a stellar salesperson and a very competent sales admin person to do the backup work. Both of those people were then working from their strengths, and both did very well for the company.

People who hire and are unaware of these kinds of conflicts are often doomed to long, unsuccessful talent searches from which they hire people who end up doing a mediocre job because of strengths conflicts.

If job descriptions are set up without any knowledge of or weight given to a person's strengths and how a person's different sets of strengths play upon each other, the hiring process will work about as well as playing darts blindfolded—you'll hit a bull's-eye now and then from sheer luck, but most of the darts won't find a scoring place in the target. The people you hire will usually not be a good fit overall for their jobs, and turnover will be higher than it should be as a result.

Those are some of the ways that a lack of strengths orientation can hurt you. Here is how having a strengths orientation can really help you.

When we perform work that we do very well, we feel genuinely happy. We feel at home with what we're doing in a deep way, and qualities such as spontaneity and creativity can more easily come forward. The product of this strong work and our attitude about it are felt and experienced in positive ways by everyone who is connected with it.

When you have a room, a department, or a company full of people all working from their strengths, everyone and everything benefits. People who love their work are happy, and happy people stick around and keep doing great things. The quality of the work is better, people get along with each other, and you'd better believe that the customers and vendors feel the difference between a happy shop and an unhappy shop.

All of which makes a huge difference to your bottom line.

When you and everyone in your company are working from your strengths and all of you are happy, the resulting efficiencies and higher performance will make your company more profitable.

So, what would a strengths-based company look like for you, and what would it take to get there?

First, develop a good job description for yourself based on your strengths. You can learn what your specific strengths are by taking the Clifton StrengthsFinder assessment from Gallup.[1] There is a short version available for just your top five strengths, but I highly recommend that you take the more detailed thirty-four strengths version instead to get all the depth and details that you need for your job description.

1. Once you have taken the assessment and have had some time to digest your strengths report, set that aside while you make a list of all the things you actually do in your position as a business owner—every large and small thing that's on your plate. What specific responsibilities and tasks do you have now, including the ones that just wiggled down over time and stuck to you? Think

_____

[1] www.gallupstrengthscenter.com/signin

of as many as you can and write them down. Take your time and list them all.

2. Now, take this responsibilities list and your list of strengths from Gallup, and spend some time with them to discover where your current responsibilities and your strengths match up and also where they don't. If you print out both lists and put them side-by-side to do this comparison, you will get a very clear picture of where the matches and mismatches are.

3. Once you have done that, make a third list, this one to combine your current tasks and responsibilities that are strengths-based and your specific strengths that each task matches up well with. This list will be the foundation of your job description.

4. Make a separate list of all the things you do that don't match up with your strengths and set it aside.

5. You need to set up your actual job description so it gives you responsibilities and tasks that reflect your strengths because that's how you will do your best version of your position. Here is the outline of a job description to give you an idea of what you're aiming for as a framework.

    - Position description:
    - Title:
    - Reports to:
    - Position summary:
    - Responsibilities and duties:
    - Strengths (Gallup) needed for optimal performance:

- Authority (authorized decision-making):
- Standards and measurements of performance:
- A typical day in this position:
- Training consists of:

It is a good idea to develop your job description with the assistance of a human resources professional to finalize the format and wording, and to check it for compliance and regulatory issues. There are many independent HR companies that can help you with this if you don't have access to in-house HR.

6. Once you have your job description laid out in alignment with your strengths, you need to deal with the list of things you've been doing that don't match your strengths. Your involvement in these activities has been holding you back, so you must give these tasks away to others for whom they *will* be a strengths match. Those tasks that are not related to strengths for you *must be strengths-based for the person to whom you give them*, or you will just be passing your strengths-conflicted performance on to someone else, and nothing good will come of that.

Imagine that each non-strength activity you are involved in is a barnacle on the bottom of your boat. Barnacles create drag and slow down a boat, and enough of them will sink it. Operating in your areas of weakness will drain you, waste your time, and yield poor results, so become *absolutely determined* to get all the barnacles—everything but your strengths-based responsibilities—off your boat. If you do this, and your people do this, your company has an extraordinary opportunity to excel and stand out above the competition. If you don't do it, your company will probably end up down in the middle with all those other companies that are succeeding at a certain level but never seem to break out.

To become strengths-based is that important to your success.

Your goal is to spend *all* your work time doing things that use your strengths because you will do better work and enjoy it more when it matches up with what you do best.

If it isn't possible for you to correlate all your tasks to your strengths immediately—you don't have enough people yet to do all the other stuff that you're not so good at, perhaps—make it a very high working priority to give away those dead spots (non-strength tasks) as soon as possible to people for whom those tasks would be aligned with their strengths.

And, set up job descriptions for every position in your company to include a list of specific strengths that are needed to perform the duties and responsibilities of each position. Use this list to help you set up interviews for applicants. Then do a Gallup Clifton StrengthsFinder assessment for each person, and only hire people who assess well for the strengths needed for their positions.

You will be amazed at how much better your organization operates when all your positions have clear job descriptions and the people who are in them all have the strengths that are needed for them.

TAKE ACTION FOR TRACTION

One thing I can do right away to start working more from my strengths is: _____

_____

_____

Another thing I will look into that might help everyone in this organization to be more strengths-based is:_____

_____

_____

People and resources I might need to make this happen are: _____

_____

_____

_____

So you've got it that job descriptions are critical for your people in order for them to color within the lines and do what they are supposed to do, but you also know that not all people problems are related to job descriptions.

HAPPY PEOPLE, HAPPY COMPANY

Some of your people may be disengaged, lazy, incompetent, gossipy, or conflict-prone. Some may not cooperate or collaborate well with each other, or they may be too competitive. They may come to you with their issues, pay little attention to your requests or advice, or actively try to torpedo ideas they don't like. Some of your people may have been right for their jobs back at the beginning but are not a good fit for their positions as they have evolved. Maybe you aren't developing people for advancement, or you don't have enough good key people at the top to run the company with you. Turnover might be more than you'd like, and hiring the right new people is a lengthy, expensive, and difficult process that often doesn't give you good results.

SCORING

Give yourself a score for how happy you currently are with your people, on a scale of 1 to 10. (1 is "I spend a lot of time putting out fires with my people," and 10 is "I have a great crew, and I am happy with how I'm doing in this area.")

Your score between 1 and 10 is _____.

THE FIX

It is impossible to have a happy workplace if there is a lot of tension or dysfunction in your workforce. There needs to be a basic level of harmony, cooperation, and trust for your workers to be able to let down their defenses enough to enjoy their work and be happy.

So, doing whatever you need to do to resolve people problems in order to have a work environment that is mostly free of friction is vitally important to the success of any efforts you might make toward enhancing happiness for your people.

If you have significant people problems that have resisted your best efforts to resolve them, you probably need an evaluation of what's working and what's not by an external consultant to clarify the situation and your options for change. You need to know exactly who is functional and happy, and who isn't and why, so you can map out the right course for improvement. Once you have evaluation results and a good plan of action, you can address specific needs.

I can tell you that companies with people problems usually also have a hiring problem. One of the biggest, most frequent issues in this area is *intuitive hiring*. This is the fairly informal process in which the business owner asks the applicant some questions from a list he made up, concludes that she seems to know what she's doing from his take on her resume, plus he gets along well with her in the interview, so he hires her. That's intuitive hiring, and it can get you into bad trouble both because you'll hire the wrong people and because your hiring isn't standardized.

You need a standardized hiring process that is based at a minimum upon a well-written job description and interviews that are *scored* for each position. A scored interview gives you ways to discover what you need to know about job candidates in a relevant, consistent, and useful way. Your intuition about a candidate should be a factor in the interview, but not the deciding factor.

Failure to use a standardized hiring process lowers the odds of good hires and also increases your legal exposure if an applicant ever challenges you about any part of your candidate evaluation or hiring process. HR can help you with this.

TAKE ACTION FOR TRACTION

One thing I can do right away to build a happier workforce is: ___

_____

_____

Another thing I will look into that might help encourage a better experience at work for my people is: _____

_____

_____

People and resources I might need to make this happen are: _____

_____

_____

I will take action by this date: _____

ELIMINATE THREE WORK HABITS THAT CAN TAKE YOU DOWN

YOU HAVE A HARD TIME LEAVING WORK AT WORK.

It's hard to keep all those balls in the air all day and then put them down at night. Getting your mind away from the office can be difficult, and may interfere with your ability to be present for and enjoy other essential parts of your life. This difficulty can take many forms.

1. *You consistently stay at the office too long.* It seems there is always something that keeps you there, something that only you can do, or something that must be done after hours, not tomorrow during the workday. This may be related to a control issue—the tendency to be too much down in the weeds with everything—or it may simply be about after hours being a quieter time to get your work done. In either case, you've probably found that your work will expand into whatever space and time you give to it, and it's hard to put it back in its box once you let it out.

2. *You take work home with you.* Rationalizing that it's easier to work uninterrupted at home, you comingle your office overflow and your private life when at home. If you have really good boundaries about it and a separate, closed-door space to do the work, you may be able to pull this off. After all, many entrepreneurs work from home all the time, so it is possible to do it while keeping some lines between your personal and work life. The temptations are many, however, and once your work camel gets his nose under your home tent, it's hard to keep the rest of him out. Let's have a cocktail while we work, let's make a personal phone call or check the laundry, or answer a homework question from a child. The list is endless and the temptations are compelling, so this way of working takes a lot of vigilance and willpower to pull off.

3. *Your mind has a hard time keeping work thoughts at bay.* While you're at your daughter's recital, a movie with your wife, dinner with friends, or watching a game on TV, or when it's time to sleep, your mind just won't stop about the business. Conceptualizing a presentation, thinking about a sales pitch, or rehashing events, new ideas, and old worries—the business camel snuffles into your mind when it's time to do other things.

SCORING

Give yourself a score for how hard or easy it is to leave work at work, on a scale of 1 to 10. (1 is "It seems as though some part of me is always tuned in to work, and it really gets in the way of my life," and 10 is "I have good boundaries about work and home life, and I am happy with how I'm doing in this area.")

Your score between 1 and 10 is _____.

THE FIX

Some of your problem may be your biology. The human mind is organized to complete things, and it will nag you with little reminders that something is not finished until you actually do it so your brain can rest or go on to the next thing. If a lot of things are undone—all those balls in the air—the poking and reminding from your brain that you need to do something about them is like a light switch that won't go off, even when you need it to.

The bad news is that your brain can become wired to overstimulation as a normal state of being if this goes on too long. The good news is that there are things you can do to keep that from happening.

The fix here is to stay focused overall, but to give your brain the breaks it needs so it can relax out of hyperdrive.

I can't overstate the need for good time management as the number one way to handle work well and leave work at work when it's time to go home.

First, it's important to know that time management is not really about time.

Time is a human-made measurement based on the movements of Earth and the sun. From those planetary movement measurements, people developed the language of "hours," "minutes," and "seconds" to name them so you and I would have a way to predictably show up together at Starbucks.

This system worked so well that the whole world now coordinates its activities based upon those measurements—or the more advanced measurements of atomic elements. Thus the "atomic clock," which sets itself to the very precise measurements of atomic element movement.

I am not just being technical about this.

Measuring heavenly objects to give us a reliable language of "time" has caused us to think of time as a thing itself, something to be managed or controlled, thus the concept of "time management."

You can't manage time, but you can manage your choices, which will then take parts of one or more "days" in your "calendar" of time to accomplish.

When you manage your choices well, the times attached to each of them will combine in ways that reflect a life and work well planned, and choice-making that works as a whole for your health and success.

People who manage choices well know that time management isn't about cramming more into the day. All of us have the same twenty-four hours each day. How we choose to use them determines how effective and happy we are.

The trap is that every activity that attracts our interest has a hidden price tag of time attached to it, and we often fail to do the simple math and add up those price tags before we make new commitments.

Let's say that I am overwhelmed at work and I spend too little time at home as a result. I get a call from the coach of my son's soccer team asking if I can help out at some weekly practices. Since I feel guilty about not having enough time at home and not spending enough time with my son, I agree. Because of the emotional weight of this decision, I might agree to do it before figuring out where I will realistically find the time two evenings a week to be at my son's soccer practice and also how that time commitment will affect all the other commitments I have already made.

The net result is that my activity choice may make my son feel better, but unless I make the right changes in my life to create the time for it, my decision could help push me toward burnout and more scheduling pressure.

A way to think about time choices that can help prevent burnout, chaos, and confusion is to consider them in the context of banking. We don't bounce checks at the bank because the bank lets us know in a big hurry when we do that, and we pay a penalty in cash for the mistake. This gives us a very clear, obvious, and painful limit on our financial spending.

We each have a bank of time that resets with a twenty-four-hour deposit every day. The problem is that no one sends us an overdraft statement or charges us a fee every time we write a bum "check" for time that we can't afford. Our punishment is real, though—we load ourselves up with ongoing stress and an overwhelmed life when our bank accounts of time are overdrawn repeatedly.

So managing time is really about managing choices and always being very clear about the time we are committing to our choices. If we want to stay sane, healthy, and happy, we must make choices that we actually have time for in our time banks.

The other big mistake we make that feeds right into this has to do with how we schedule our time.

Many of us see those time blocks marching forward one after another in our calendars, so we follow the blocks and schedule ourselves back-to-back right on through the day. If those time blocks were cars, they'd all be driving six inches from the next car's bumper at eighty miles an hour. What happens if the lead car has to slow down fast? There's a big crash and a big mess. In your calendar, your day goes fine until one event hangs up, and then all the blocks behind that event get crunched because there's no room to make schedule adjustments.

The answer is to book some gaps into your day. I usually recommend a half-hour gap in the morning and another half hour in the afternoon—spaces when you don't schedule anything ahead of time, no matter how tempted you are to do so. Those gaps are there to give you options when your schedule blows up on you, and you'll be amazed at how much better you'll feel at the end of the day, knowing both that the gaps are there and how effective they are when you have to actually use them for damage control. If you don't have to use your gaps for that purpose, you can use them instead to catch up on work, put on your sneakers and go for a walk, or even catch a little couch nap.

The last and most important time management element is about how to prioritize. Because we have so many choices in life today, we need our prioritization to be simple and clear.

Here is how to set some simple priorities:

#1 Priority: High Impact. If you could have a shot at a contract to double your sales or hire a game-changing professional to be your operations manager, or if the IRS wanted to audit you, these would all be high-impact events, and they would deserve your highest priority. Note that their top priority ranking doesn't come from the fact that they are positive or negative events but rather that they will have a high impact upon you and your business.

#2 Priority: Oil the Machine. These are the priorities that keep things going—things that, if they're not done, will throw sand in the gears. Making payroll on time every month, scheduling time to get to know your employees better, or giving them meaningful performance bonuses are examples of things that aren't dramatic, but they keep oil in the machine. Keep an eye on these to spot any items that might need to be moved from Oil the Machine to High Impact priority.

#3 Priority: Triage the Noise. Everything that doesn't obviously fit either of the top priorities is noise. This is all the stuff that happens or wants to happen in your day that may or may not be important. You've got to triage the noise—sort out nuggets of importance from all the noise, and then let the rest go. Use the first two priorities to determine whether or not noise is just noise.

There's a lot more to time management—I often do half-day or full-day trainings about it—but these are some of the most important basics that will have a positive impact on your happiness and your experience of life when you use them.

TAKE ACTION FOR TRACTION:

One thing I can do right away to better manage my choices and my time is:_____

_____

_____

Another thing I will look into that might help is:_____

_____

_____

_____

People and resources I might need to make this happen are: _____

_____

_____

_____

I will take action by this date: _____

YOU NEED BALANCE TO MOVE FORWARD

You have problems with work/life imbalance. Too much time at work can create a deficit of time at home, yet you are hooked into this imbalance by the feeling that there aren't enough hours in a day to do what needs to be done. This makes you feel as though you have to stay at work until you can at least make a meaningful dent in your to-do list, which never seems to get shorter. No calendar can contain your work; it's a torrent of demands that never ends.

Since your people follow your lead, you end up creating a company culture of boundary-busters where schedules are routinely trashed, plans are just wishes, your people can never depend on getting home on time, and—starting with you—people don't keep their commitments, so there's a real whiff of chaos in the air. Workplace happiness isn't a real possibility in this environment.

SCORING

Give yourself a score for how hard or easy it is to balance your work and your personal life, on a scale of 1 to 10. (1 is "I never get home on time, and I've forgotten how old my kids are," and 10 is "Work and home life are pretty well balanced, and I am happy with how I'm doing in this area.")

Your score between 1 and 10 is _____.

THE FIX

Good time management is the first part of the fix for this problem. Doing what needs to be done more efficiently in less time would certainly contribute to more balance between your work and your personal life, but there's more to it than that.

Work/life imbalance is, on the face of it, about the amount of time you spend at work compared to the time you spend at home. For most people, the problem is commonly about spending too much time at work. Determined people who want to change this dynamic often make big efforts to equalize the time spent at work and at home, yet it isn't unusual for them to report that they still don't feel any better even though their time spent at each place is more balanced.

A lack of *inner/outer balance* is probably the culprit in that case.

Inner/outer balance is about how much time you spend doing for yourself, as opposed to time spent doing for others.

A typical example scenario is that you run through your busy day at work, and then you also run through your busy time at home, taking care of the needs of job, kids, spouse, and chores before the day is done. The amount of time between work and home may be balanced, but if you are super busy supporting others in both places and there's no time left for you and your own personal needs, that's a problem.

We can't physically breathe out, out, out, and keep breathing out without an in-breath and expect to live. We would literally, physically, die.

A life of constant activity geared toward others both at work and at home leaves no room for your in-breath—time for you to recharge and fill up—and an important part of you that needs to breathe in that way doesn't get to do it.

Meeting your important personal needs, as well as the needs of people and situations out in the world, is what inner/outer balance is about.

We need both work/life balance and inner/outer balance, coupled with good choices and time management, in order to have lives that work and feel good.

This all sounds complicated, and it can be.

It used to be that work was over at five o'clock. You went home, ate dinner, and spent time with your family, and then you probably had a little time sitting on the porch or reading a book before bed.

Life has changed for most of us and those days are gone, but if you can create habits and rituals at your home that are equivalent to those pacing and relaxation levels, you and your family will be a lot healthier and happier.

Inner/outer life balance happens when you *schedule* the time to do things you want to do for yourself, as well as scheduling the time you spend doing things for and with others. I don't recommend to-do lists, because they mean, "When I get around to it." Schedule what you really want to get done; most of us take a scheduled appointment much more seriously than a to-do item.

For example, I schedule my work, but I also schedule in my calendar to go fishing, to go to lunch regularly with my friends, and to go away to write books in peace and quiet. My wife schedules her work, and she also schedules hanging out with her friends, playing and working with horses, eating meals out by herself, and holing up for quiet time with books and her iPad.

Whatever it would look like for you, the activities you pick don't have to be big, take a lot of time, or cost much in order to have a really positive effect on your inner/outer balance. The key is simply to spend time on yourself regularly doing activities that are revitalizing and feel good to you.

TAKE ACTION FOR TRACTION:

One thing I can do right away to have better work/life and inner/outer balance is:_____

_____

_____

Another thing I will look into that might help is: _____

_____

_____

_____

People and resources I might need to make this happen are: _____

_____

_____

_____

I will take action by this date: _____

GOOD STRESS, BAD STRESS

You feel overwhelmed and stressed too much of the time. Your fitness isn't what you'd like it to be, your temper flares too easily, and you often feel tired, even after adequate sleep. The doc made a face about your test numbers the last time, and you have fantasies of getting away for a while, but you find it nearly impossible to do so.

It seems that everyone wants more pieces of you than you've got, both at home and at work. Time flies, and when you finally get to bed at night, sleep can be elusive.

Your mood, underneath everything else, is a bit blue.

SCORING

Give yourself a score for how stressed you are, on a scale of 1 to 10. (1 is "I am really stressed and my life is a blur," and 10 is "I have a good balance between stress and relaxation in my work and in my life, and I am happy with how I'm doing in this area.")

Your score between 1 and 10 is _____.

THE FIX

It is a well-known fact that high *ongoing* levels of stress will impair your health and ability to function in a lot of ways. Owning a business can cause monster stress, and if that's how it is for you and you don't want to crash and burn, you need to start a strong *self-care routine* that will break up the continuous stress.

Short-term stress, however, can be good for us, according to a Stanford University study, and the ability to view short-term stress as a necessary, time-limited investment with a good outcome will lessen its negative effects.

Let's strategize, though, about long-term stress—the kind that's not good—since so many of us experience it that way.

It's interesting how easily we recognize and meet the need for maintenance for our cars, but it's hard for us to generate the same watchfulness and willingness to take care of ourselves. It's too easy in today's world for the busy, noisy demands of life to drown out the quieter, important needs of body, mind, and spirit.

Self-care—taking care of the self—includes doing everything you need to do to take good care of all the parts of you. As a practice, it means doing things to actively promote your physical, mental, emotional, and spiritual well-being.

Stress reduction is specifically about lowering or removing unwanted, ongoing stress in your life, and it needs to be part of your overall self-care practice. Read the excellent book *Why Zebras Don't Get Ulcers* by Robert M. Sapolsky to learn more about how ongoing stress affects you and what you can do about it.

TAKE CARE OF YOURSELF PHYSICALLY:

- Move. For at least thirty minutes a day, get up and move until your body is involved with what you're doing. Don't sit for more than thirty minutes without taking a break. Start and maintain an exercise program of some kind and stick to it.

- Put good fuel in your body and stay clear of junk food. Learn the difference between good food and junk food—read nutrition labels and practice portion control. If there were just one book you would want to read about this, it is: *Eat, Drink and Be Healthy: The Harvard Medical School Guide to Healthy Eating*.

- Realize that any diet that makes you feel as though you're in food jail won't work. You have to enjoy your healthy meals and not starve yourself, or you will slip right back into unhealthy ones. You might want to try the rule of 75/25. If 75% of what you eat is good, clean food, there's probably room in the other 25% to have a chocolate chip cookie or some ice cream now and then. That way, you're not in food jail and you can mostly maintain your food integrity.

TAKE CARE OF YOURSELF MENTALLY:

- Your brain is the most complex organ in your body. It controls what your body does and how healthy you are mentally. Here's a book that will help you to understand your brain and how to take care of it: *Brain Rules: 12 Principles for Surviving and Thriving at Work, Home and School,* by John Medina.

TAKE CARE OF YOURSELF EMOTIONALLY:

- The physical health of your brain has a lot to do with how well you function emotionally, and many emotional difficulties have been discovered to be rooted in brain chemistry. Some mental health issues are chemical disorders, not just freestanding moods or emotional patterns. Depression, anxiety, and sleep disorders are examples of problems that have a strong chemical component. Here's a great book by Dr. Judith Orloff that talks about how to find and maintain healthy emotional balance: *Emotional Freedom: Liberate Yourself from Negative Emotions and Transform Your Life.*

TAKE CARE OF YOURSELF SPIRITUALLY:

- *Spirit* as a word refers to the essence of something, and to be spiritual is to be curious and inquisitive about how our deepest essence-of-self connects to everything else. When we are feeling a need to learn more about this, we often talk about it in terms of wanting to find our purpose or looking for the meaning of life.

Seeking purpose and meaning in life is a spiritual journey, whether religion—the celebration of spirituality—ever gets involved in it or not.

You don't have to be spiritually curious, and you don't have to go to church to be spiritual, but for a lot of people it helps. For others, deep meaning is found in daily living, and their church is wherever they find or celebrate a strong sense of meaning and connection with life.

In the context of self-care, it is important that you pay attention to whatever you see as your spiritual self as well as the parts of your life where you have an opportunity to express it. If you do have a spiritual inclination, don't let it get lost in the daily routines, and don't compromise its integrity by your actions.

If you don't have a spiritual itch, remember to celebrate what you see as right and good in life. Business leadership can grind on you because you see so much of people's not-so-good stuff sometimes that it can be hard to remember to celebrate the good. Celebrate what's right in the world—in your world and the world—or you will forget it and will become unable to see it, and your life will lose its zest and color.

TAKE ACTION FOR TRACTION:

One thing I can do right away to improve my self-care is:_____

_____

_____

_____

Another thing I will look into that might help is:_____

_____

_____

_____

People and resources I might need to make this happen are: _____

_____

_____

_____

I will take action by this date: _____

CHAPTER 10

WHAT TO DO WHEN YOU'RE NOT HITTING YOUR PLAN

You were really careful getting into this business venture. You were very clear that you were taking on the substantial risks of an entrepreneurial business in exchange for a substantially

> ANOTHER REASON PEOPLE BECOME ENTREPENEURS:
>
> **ENTREPRENEURS HAVE FINANCIAL AND LIFESTYLE GOALS THEY WANT TO ACHIEVE THAT WON'T HAPPEN IN A JOB.**

greater payoff down the road. You worked up a set of goals, did an analysis of the business you were getting into, and worked with a lot of scenarios and planning before you pulled the trigger. You did everything you could to launch this business right.

And then stuff happened.

A distressed entrepreneur—we'll call him Stan—called me for a consult one day. He told me his lifetime dream had been to own and run a successful publication of some kind and make good money with it. When the opportunity came his way to purchase a monthly magazine, he jumped on it. He had lots of great ideas, a good general grasp of the market, and some money to invest in spiffing up the product. Things went well for about three years, and the magazine grew fast. But year four, revenues were flat.

The same thing for year five—there was no growth in subscribers or advertising revenues for that year, either.

Stan was making a living at the time, but nowhere near a killing. He wasn't within shouting distance of his goals of dominating his niche in his region and making big money. His publication required huge amounts of his time, and he was stuck at a point where he couldn't quite afford to hire the next tier of people who would fill in some gaps and take a significant piece of the daily load off of him.

It was starting to eat at Stan that the rewards weren't showing up yet. Flat revenues weren't going to do it.

When he first considered buying the business, Stan did a market analysis to assure himself that the customers were there for the changes he wanted to make to the publication. He was progressive in his political and social views, and so were the magazine's readers. His magazine content was oriented that way, too, but he lived in a very conservative state, so he wanted to be sure there were enough progressive readers to support the growth he wanted. The region was economically sound when he began, and the people who were in his target demographic were moving into the region at that time in large numbers.

The inflow of those demographically ideal new residents was predicted to steadily increase over time, but it slowed instead. A tough national economy and a less-than-rosy employment forecast reduced the stream of Stan's new readers to a trickle.

Stan was doing everything right with the other parts of his business model and the basics of his publication, but he didn't have enough readers or potential readers yet to support his ultimate revenue projections, which, once he accomplished them, would make possible the achievement of his own personal work and financial goals.

He could choose to run the magazine at its current level, which would at least make him a living, but it might not take him where he really wanted to go. He bought it to break out into bigger success, not to just survive in another job, so he wondered what he could do in this difficult situation and what his options were.

If you are in a similarly difficult situation in which any of the following are happening, what do you think your options are?

- Your business is underperforming to expectations.
- There is an unsatisfactory level of profitability.
- Increasing costs of doing business are eating into profits.
- More owner funding for the business is needed.
- The time line for your personal goal fulfillment is getting longer.
- The business you envisioned morphs into something else—a small business turns big, a big business gets small, or products and services have changed.
- You're chained to your desk, and your lifestyle needs are not being met.

SCORING

Give yourself a score for how much or little business success issues are influencing your work and your personal life, on a scale of 1 to 10. (1 is "I worry about things like this a lot, and that really gets in the way of my happiness," and 10 is "My business is on track, and I am happy with how I'm doing in this area.")

Your score between 1 and 10 is _____.

THE FIX

Stan and I came up with a plan for his business that looked like this.

Since the problem-specific fixes he had come up with just weren't working well, he needed to review and re-vision his business as a whole. He started by asking himself the following questions and writing down the answers. I asked him not to judge those answers—it's unrealistic, too little too late, crazy, revenues don't support it—because sometimes the smallest snippet of a weird idea is the germ of a solution. As you answer these questions for *your* business, let your imagination run free and write down all incoming ideas.

- What needs to happen that's not happening?
- What is happening that needs to stop?
- What does this situation tell you about the company's strengths and weaknesses?
- What does it tell you as a leader about your strengths and weaknesses (no beating yourself up allowed)?
- How could you expand upon your strengths—upon any part of the situation that is working well? It is sometimes easier to build upon strength than it is to fix weakness.

- Are there changes you need to make to your business model?
- Do any changes need to happen regarding the people who work for you?
- What are the smallest changes you could make that would produce the biggest positive results?
- What kind of help do you need in order to introduce a different perspective to your picture and innovate some additional solutions? Might it be time to get some outside analysis and assistance?
- Is it time to adjust your goals? (Start with the end goal and work backward.)
- What resources do you need in order to improve this situation?

In Stan's case, we went through his answers to the above questions, and several helpful ideas came to him during that process.

1. The core magazine might take more time to find its growth again, but in the meantime he could spin off a series of guides and directories for his readership market. This would give him additional products to sell, and they would also be good marketing tools to attract people who were unfamiliar with the magazine.

2. Stan knew of other magazines like his around the United States, so he decided to host a meeting of their publishers. He had an idea that, as a group, they could start a national section in their individual regional publications where they would carry articles and advertising from each other's magazines. This would, in effect, give each individual magazine national exposure, readership, and advertising. Stan followed through, and this alliance opened up an additional revenue stream for the magazines that participated.

The most important thing Stan learned, though, was how to generate good, profitable ideas in challenging times. Our coaching collaboration gave him time and space to regain his creativity and hopefulness, and the ideas just started coming.

This worked for Stan, but if you find yourself reluctant to do this exercise or to dig into possible changes, it could be that you've already had enough and that your reluctance is telling you that you need to move on to something else.

Even if that's not the case, it can sometimes help during tough or disappointing times to set up an exit strategy for the future—a "That's it, I quit" plan that is tied to a trigger event such as a certain amount of cash depletion or the inability to achieve specific goals by certain dates. Making an agreement with yourself that you will only continue in a difficult situation to a certain point, defining specifically what that point is, and then setting up a practical get-out strategy as a backup can take some weight off and reenergize you to come back at your situation refreshed. When you know that the problem has a limit in the future, you have more energy and ideas about it in the present.

Also, find ways to enjoy whatever level of success you've had or currently have. These ups and downs are all part of your education for greater success if you can see them that way. Many of my clients find that they achieve great success at some point, but that it often comes with a longer timetable and more excursions down side roads than they originally expected. Most highly successful entrepreneurs are serial entrepreneurs—they've been up on the business horse and fallen off a number of times before they finally get to ride.

When interviewed for a recent book, many big-time entrepreneurs independently identified the biggest single factor for their success as *persistence*.

TAKE ACTION FOR TRACTION:

One thing I can do right away to contribute to my business success in a small or large way is:_____

_____

_____

Another thing I will look into that might help is:_____

_____

_____

People and resources I might need to make this happen are: _____

_____

_____

I will take action by this date: _____

CHAPTER 11

THE TROUBLE WITH BEING THE BOSS

One of the first things you find out when you open your business as an entrepreneur is that you still have bosses, even when you are self-employed.

> ANOTHER REASON PEOPLE BECOME ENTREPENEURS:
>
> **ENTREPRENEURS KNOW THEY AREN'T CUT OUT TO WORK FOR OTHER PEOPLE.**

Anyone who has control over whether you work and how you do your work is a boss to some degree. If you are a formerly employed person who thought you were free of supervision when you walked away from the job boss and opened your own shop, you quickly learned otherwise.

A partial list of people who function as some kind of "boss" in their role with you includes:

- Federal, state, and local regulators
- Taxing entities

- Your attorney
- Your accountant
- Professional ethics boards
- Your board of directors, if you have one
- Your investors, banker, and other lenders
- Your family

In a sense, you are working in some way for all these people. You are accountable to them and must conform to what they want from you in order to be in business. At times, it may feel as though a whole lot of people get to pull your strings and tell you what to do!

SCORING

Give yourself a score for how well you work with people in positions of authority relative to your business, on a scale of 1 to 10. (1 is "Their demands really get in the way of my happiness," and 10 is "I am happy with how I'm doing in this area.")

Your score between 1 and 10 is _____.

THE FIX

If you're cranky because of all this bossing around that you receive from people who have a say in how you run your business, it might actually seem simple, looking back, to have had just one boss for everything. But you're in it now with this business of yours, and you must find the freedoms in running it that offset the realities of your obligations to everyone else if you are to be happy.

The most fundamental freedom you have is the freedom to see this situation from any perspective you choose, and you have a couple of basic perspective choices here: to see yourself as controlled by others and resent it, or to collaborate wherever possible with external authorities so needs get met on both sides as easily as possible and you can go on your way.

You will never be completely free from the control of others—it's just not possible. From the nurse who smacked your bottom when you were born to the funeral director who facilitates your exit from this world, your life is constantly involved with the necessity of dealing with others in positions of authority. Learning how to do that well is a huge priority for a business leader.

And, there's another interesting possibility here that may be going on for you.

If you don't like being under the authority of a boss and have spent a lot of time in that position, you can have big problems when you become one yourself. You may have so thoroughly disliked being on the receiving end of the boss experience that you fear becoming the boss you didn't like.

When you take on your own business and you have employees, you become the boss, like it or not. Knowing how to be a good one can be a total mystery for a variety of reasons until you learn how it's done, especially if your past experiences with bosses were not good.

In this scenario of becoming a boss and not yet knowing how to do it, most business owners will, without realizing it, imitate the bosses they have known in the past. If you've had good bosses, you will have some good leadership clues to work from. If the previous boss was a bad one, you may tend to imitate that, too, whether you realize it or not.

Faced with a lack of leadership skills in the beginning, it can be easy to reach for whatever you know from the past that will fill in for them.

It is also useful to consider how you define the word boss. I've used that word here previously, but to be a boss is mostly about telling people what to do. Move that lumber over here, call these fifty sales leads, do this, do that. Telling—bossing—is one form of leadership and is a necessary part of it, but you need to be more than that when it's your job to move a whole company forward. You need to know how to motivate people to follow you, and then you must be able to guide them to their success—give them a clear vision of where you are all going together and what their piece of that success looks like. Then, when they succeed, they will have carried your company to success. That is the core of what leadership is really about.

If you've been bossing instead of leading, you've got an opportunity to make a big leap forward here.

For some people, leadership abilities come naturally, but even natural leaders have to learn specific leadership skills to get people at different levels to perform well. When you lead, you also have to be visible and accountable to other people in new and specific ways. You must supply vision, define the mission, and know how a business operates in the way a mechanic knows all about an engine so you can know what you're looking at when you see your business unfold and grow before your eyes. Above all, you must be good with people—your workers, your customers, and your vendors.

It is possible to become a leader if you've been more of a boss in the past. Keep in mind, however, that they are different roles. You may need to do some learning specifically about what goes into leadership so you can separate that out from old habits that came with being a boss.

Here are some of the differences:

BOSSES:

1. Tell instead of asking
2. Push instead of pulling
3. Assume they know the answers
4. Demand obedience and conformity
5. Punish failure
6. Reward compliance
7. View workers as replaceable parts
8. Exhibit attitudes of superiority and entitlement

LEADERS:

1. Ask as well as tell
2. Pull as well as push
3. Know that the wisdom of a group will sometimes exceed the wisdom of individuals, no matter their rank
4. Require engagement, high performance, and real contributions from their workers

5. Use failures to teach about success

6. Reward innovation and working smart

7. View workers as valued members of a team

8. Exhibit attitudes of strength, openness, and encouragement

When it comes to heading up a company, leadership has far greater benefits than behaving like a boss:

- People stick around because they enjoy their work.

- Workers are free to innovate and contribute as much as they can instead of just being cogs in a machine.

- A real leader inspires passion in his or her people, and passion-infused work is superior to just-working-for-a-paycheck work, both in how it is performed and in its results.

- Everybody knows where they are going at all levels; there is a unified approach among the various people and parts of the business.

- Good leaders hold everyone, including themselves, accountable to the same standards of excellence. They are fair, and workers respond to fairness with loyalty and trust.

- Companies that have excellent leadership operate better internally and externally, which brings more profit to the bottom line.

The benefits are clear—so how can you learn more about leadership?

Many entrepreneurs don't have a formal business education; they just dive in and run their companies as well as they can, and that is often very well indeed. If you are one of those business leaders who learned mostly in the School of Experience and Hard Knocks, here is some reading that might be useful to organize and add to what you have already learned.

Peter Drucker, one of the founding gurus of modern business, has combined three of his books into one: *The Executive in Action: Managing for Results, Innovation and Entrepreneurship,* and *The Effective Executive.*

Another high-value step you could take is to hire an executive coach. Executive coaches give company leaders a neutral sounding board for their ideas and decisions, and they ask leaders insight-producing questions that lead to good decision making. Also, it is lonely at the top, and it is helpful for leaders to have someone to talk to confidentially who knows business and who doesn't have an agenda about them or their companies.

TAKE ACTION FOR TRACTION:

One thing I can do right away to contribute to my sense of business wisdom is: _____

_____

Another thing I will look into that might help is:_____

_____

_____

People and resources I might need to make this happen are: _____

_____

_____

I will take action by this date: _____

CHAPTER 12

THE FREEDOM OF SELF-EMPLOYMENT

Entrepreneurs want unlimited potential—they want freedom and autonomy.

When you are an entrepreneur at heart, it is natural that you

> ANOTHER REASON PEOPLE BECOME ENTREPENEURS:
>
> **ENTREPRENEURS HAVE A DESIRE FOR FREEDOM AND AUTONOMY.**

would chafe at restrictions imposed upon you by others. *Freedom* isn't just a word for you—it's an operational necessity. Freedom has two different aspects that need to work together, though, for entrepreneurs to be successful and happy.

The first is that they must *feel* free and experience their days and their work as being full of free choices. The second is that entrepreneurs must actually *be* mostly free of what they judge to be *unnecessary* or *unacceptable* limitations on their work and their potential. These limitations will cause a loss of that precious feeling of daily freedom if they persist.

If you are an entrepreneurial accountant, for instance, working with numbers all day in your own business for your own clients, you will experience great freedom because you work for yourself and you are free to work as you wish. If, on the other hand, the IRS starts imposing unreasonably broad and restrictive rules on how accountants do business—something many accountants will tell you is actually happening these days—their daily feeling of freedom may diminish under the weight of those external rules because they view themselves and their potential as unduly restricted.

Areas where entrepreneurs often start feeling cramped in their potential and their freedoms include:

- Time
- Money
- Competition
- High-impact business setbacks—recessions, market changes, low sales
- Regulation
- Personal energy
- Negativity at work

There is also a matter of psychological happiness that is involved here.

In a psychologically happy and healthy person, there is a balance between the urge for total freedom to do as one pleases and the necessary acceptance of fair levels of external control or regulation. This person is okay with the necessity for restrictions and boundaries to some degree in all areas of life as long as there is enough freedom in the mix to make the limitations worthwhile.

The ability to find this balance is usually determined by our nature as individuals and by our history—what we have each experienced about freedom and boundaries in the past. These factors shape our responses to limitations in life.

If we have a freedom-loving, exploring nature, the freedoms of entrepreneurship may be a right and natural extension of that part of our nature, and we may then be comfortable with our limits. If we have experienced times of restriction and loss of freedom—years at a demanding job we didn't like, for example—we will need work that feels really free when we come out of that bad job, and we will likely be very sensitive to restrictions.

Although the achievement of freedom is one of the deepest and most common motivations expressed by people who are drawn to entrepreneurial business, actually having the freedom to do what you want and doing it your way within the structured needs of a business is a difficult dance.

Many entrepreneurs have a temperament that could be expressed on the Revolutionary War battle flag—"Don't Tread on Me." They are ready to do business their way, and they have strong ideas about what that means. Most of them think they will find more freedom in business ownership than they would be able to have in working for others. This is true in some important and satisfying ways, but every choice in life has its trade-offs, and there are many other lessons embedded in the pursuit of freedom.

When you are employed, you pretty much know when you're working and when you're off. You know the parameters of the job itself—what you do and what you don't do. You know how much freedom you have, both in the ways you can perform your work and in how much time is yours away, because those freedoms already exist within a framework created by someone else.

The template of your work life is someone else's that you must follow, not one you created.

The biggest challenge for entrepreneurs is that there is no template—no set of dance steps on the floor to follow. All the choices are yours, at least initially, and this amounts to so much freedom that it needs structure and limits to make sense. You must define who does what when, and how they do it, including you and your role in the company. You define thousands of details about your business, and the result is your company template that others follow, within which you also have your freedoms and your limitations as the business owner.

It is easy to imagine the freedom of working for yourself when you are working for someone else. When you actually start working for yourself, though, you quickly learn about the demands of a business that will eat you whole if you let them, and about how to maintain a sense of freedom and autonomy even when you're in the grip of the overload.

You may be very aware that freedom has its complexities, and you may have decided to start the simplest of businesses, one with a bare minimum of structure and complication to it, but if you are reading this book you have employees or contract workers, and things are a lot more complicated now.

SCORING

Give yourself a score for how free you feel in the performance of your business and the freedom you have when you're away from it, on a scale of 1 to 10. (1 is "I'm running as fast as I can to keep up with my business every day," and 10 is "I have just the right balance of involvement and freedom in my business.")

Your score between 1 and 10 is _____.

THE FIX

Some definitions might help at this point.

Freedom – The power or right to act, speak, or think as one wants without hindrance or restraint

Autonomy – Freedom from external control or influence; independence

Here is something you may have thought of, but perhaps not exactly in this way: once you have your business template in place, that business becomes an entity, and every entity has needs of its own, many of which require your attention in ways you didn't think of in the beginning. When people are first attracted to entrepreneurship, they often imagine getting to the part of having a business that allows them their freedoms—the payoff in time and money to live a good life outside of the business. They usually find out as they get into it that this part of their dream comes to fruition later, after what can be a hard and long "grow your business" time that precedes the "we get to have our reward now" time.

Having your own business is a lot like having your own kid.

The child prodigy who is mature beyond his or her years is a rare kid. What most parents get instead is a very messy and all-over-the-map child experience. The gigantic rolling tumbleweed of parenthood consumes huge amounts of parental energy and time for all those years until maturity seeps into the situation.

The same is true of most entrepreneurial businesses.

A very low number of folks will start a business and have quick success that follows a solid upward arc. And, some may have big, free-ranging lives outside of work even while running their businesses, but I don't know many of those people.

Most entrepreneurs—you freedom-loving, autonomous entrepreneurs—get some kind of immersion experience with business ownership that's a lot like raising a kid. This is true whether the business succeeds, struggles, or fails. That business becomes a living thing with its own needs, and you are the default provider of a lot of those needs, whether you like it or not.

This is where a lot of business owners start to feel claustrophobic instead of free and autonomous.

The trick is that you need to learn how to feel free and do things your way within the more structured environment that may be happening right now, just for a while, and to be happy with that version of freedom and autonomy until it gets bigger. If you do your business right, that prosperous independent business-owner life is a real possibility further down the road, but you have to go through the first four of the seven stages of business development to get there.

THE SEVEN STEPS OF AN ENTREPRENEUR'S BUSINESS

STEP ONE:

The Idea (What to do with your Great Business Idea)

Biggest challenge: Knowing what you need to know before deciding whether or not to start a business

STEP TWO:

Ready, Set, Go (Setting up and opening your business)

Biggest challenge: Inadequate planning and preparation

STEP THREE:

Viability (Ongoing survival)

Biggest challenge: Making ongoing sales to support basic expenses and needs

STEP FOUR:

Targeted Growth (Grow to thrive)

Biggest challenge: Coordinating all parts of your business so they grow together

STEP FIVE:

Real Business (Owner independence)

Biggest challenge: Getting key people, systems, and infrastructure in place so you don't have to be present

STEP SIX:

Grow Big (Scale up)

Biggest challenge: Having enough cash and borrowing power

STEP SEVEN:

Niche Dominance (Achievement of goals, abundant cash, and revenues)

Biggest challenge: Getting stale and slow; growing away from core strengths

When you reach step five, the train that has the big payoff for all your hard work will pull into the station. The rewards get bigger and more frequent starting here. This happens because you have a *real business,* and here's how I define that term:

1. *Your business functions well without your presence.* You can be away for a day, a week, or a year, and the business rolls on without the need for you to be there. Your time is your own—you have achieved time freedom.

2. *You have all the resources you need to support the personal life you want outside of work.* You can live the life you really want, whatever that looks like. You have financial freedom.

3. *Your business can be sold for a good profit, if and when you want to do that.* Some entrepreneurs can't imagine ever selling their companies, but should the day ever come when that might be desirable, your business is substantial enough to sell at a good price. You have the freedom to choose whether or not to be business-focused anymore.

Once those three things are true, your business is no longer eating you up unless you choose to let it do so, and you are free to step back and shape your life so you can live much more of it your way.

A *real* business supports your needs and does not require your continuing contribution or attention.

The first step toward having a real business is to start where you are and redefine how you can feel free and be autonomous within the structure and demands of your business *as it is now* while you work to build the business you want at the more advanced business stage where you want to be.

If your ideal life is about taking vacations and traveling the world, for example, maybe a smaller piece of that lifestyle would do for now. Perhaps you can take a series of shorter trips, even long weekends, and maybe doing that will fulfill your vacation and travel lifestyle hunger just enough until the fuller version arrives.

In that spirit, here are some ways to redesign the life you live now in a way that acknowledges your current business commitments while at the same time giving you enough of your dream so you feel free and autonomous overall:

1. *Define your ideal life.* If I handed you a magic wand, what is the life you would create with it if there were no limits? What would it look like? What is the life that fulfills the dream you had when you decided to become an entrepreneur? If you didn't have a long-term dream that was very specific and it's been something more like "being free to travel" or "taking more time to be together," now is the time to get specific. Travel where? Be

together to do what? Bring all the elements of that dream to clear, detailed life and write them down so the dream feels like something real, not just a gauzy generality. Exactly what will your dream look like when you are living it? Capture that.

2. *Look at the elements of your dream* (travel and being together, in our example) and ask yourself, "What could I/we do now that would hit that desire—something smaller, perhaps, that would give me/us some satisfaction about it right now?" Sometimes you don't need to eat a whole big ice-cream cone; a couple of bites might suffice for now. Write down what you come up with for each element of your dream—the things you can do now or very soon to satisfy some of those desires—and start building those things into your current life. They will grow over time.

3. *Use strategic planning* to embed these dream tastes into your life. The French writer, poet, aristocrat, journalist, and pioneering aviator Antoine de Saint-Exupéry long ago summed up the need for strategic planning this way: "A goal without a plan is just a wish."

Businesspeople think of strategic planning as purely a business tool, but it can be much bigger than that. Every spring, my wife and I go away to a condo, where we each do an updated strategic plan for our businesses, plus we do one together for our marriage. The type of strategic planning we do is different and more effective than the usual business strategic planning.

- *Start with the finish line and work backward from that.* Whatever your goals are, start with what it looks like and feels like to have reached each one, and then reverse-engineer from those a detailed vision for the steps you need to take to get to it. If you start with the completed goal and work backward, those steps will pop out and become quite obvious to you.

- *Break down each step into specific actions* you will take, and put those actions into a monthly or quarterly time line in your calendar. Without a written calendar time line, this whole process will likely fall by the wayside and fail. What are the items and projects you will need to address? Write them down and schedule them.

A note about planning: The best-laid plans often don't happen in straight lines, so don't expect your plan to unfold perfectly in reality the way it is on paper. A strategic planning document is a living, changing thing, so you will need to review it periodically to see what needs updating.

TAKE ACTION FOR TRACTION:

One thing I can do right away to have more freedom, even while running my business, is: _____

_____

_____

Another thing I will look into that might help is:_____

_____

_____

People and resources I might need to make this happen are: _____

_____

_____

I will take action by this date: _____

CHAPTER 13

EVERYTHING NEEDS SOME CONTROL, BUT HOW MUCH IS TOO MUCH?

Being in control of our own destinies is one of the strongest reasons we choose entrepreneurship, but the downsides of exerting too much control are very

> ANOTHER REASON PEOPLE BECOME ENTREPENEURS:
>
> **ENTREPRENEURS NEED TO BE IN CONTROL— TO BE IN CHARGE OF WHAT'S HAPPENING.**

destructive. Control is a good thing until it's not. It's your business, after all, and if you want to run it your way, that's fair enough. But, if "your way" extends into every nook and cranny of things and there's no room for other people to contribute some of their way, you'll be known as a control freak—a bad boss who demands rather than leads.

It is so easy in the beginning of your business to wear too many hats and have your fingers in too many pies. Until a company is big enough to be fully staffed, the owner may have to sell, keep the books, help answer the phones, and micromanage new, inexperienced workers. All of this is normal, but it can become a big happiness reducer if it goes on too long. If you still feel as though you have to control everything that's important, even when you finally have good people to handle those things, it's time to take a deep breath and step back.

A tremendous amount of anxiety can come up when you run a business, questions in your mind about how well you are handling it, and nervousness about what lies ahead. Sometimes you're not even aware of it, but this nervousness can pull you into feeling the need to be involved in everything, just to be sure it's all done right.

Our first human instinct when anxiety arises is to try to manage events into submission so the anxiety goes away.

Sometimes applying a lot of control works and is just what is needed, at least temporarily. The key, though, is to recognize the effective limits of control when you hit them and dial it back before it becomes a habit that hurts more than it helps. If you don't do that, the anxiety that the control is trying to eliminate returns because nobody can control everything all the time.

If you can't moderate your need to control, this can lead to resentments and clashes between you and your people, a "yes-man (or woman)" culture where people are only free to agree with you, a lack of innovation and leadership except for yours, a lack of collaboration and cooperation, turf wars, high turnover, and a tense and obviously unhappy workplace.

SCORING

Give yourself a score for how much you have a need to control and be in charge, on a scale of 1 to 10. (1 is "I do control a lot, but if I didn't, things wouldn't get done," and 10 is "I exert just the right amount of control to draw the lines, and my people get things done within those lines. I am happy with how I'm doing in this area.")

Your score between 1 and 10 is _____.

THE FIX

The answer is to learn to let go and evolve into being a boss who trusts and supports other people to do their work instead of micro-managing or doing their work for them.

I know, it's easier said than done.

Many people who overcontrol aren't aware of it or won't admit it, but here's a list of ten behaviors that could give you an idea of where you stand, somewhere between giving away all control and taking on too much of it.

You might have a tendency toward overcontrol at work if:

- People don't react well to your "constructive criticism"
- You are the first to offer solutions to perceived problems
- You "help" a lot, offering unsolicited suggestions for professional and personal improvement
- You have rituals and set ways of doing things
- You don't trust your people to do as good a job as you
- You withhold attention from people to get them to fall in line with your expectations

- It is very hard for you to allow others to be upset with you or disagree with you
- You play favorites among your people
- You are uncomfortable with unknowns—there should be an answer for everything
- You usually dominate conversations
- You do not encourage feedback

There is not a score for this section; it's meant more to be an informal self-evaluation. If you have a feeling that you are a fit for any of these, here are some gentle correctives you can try.

It is ultimately exhausting to be the source of all solutions. Practice asking your people for solutions related to their work areas before offering your suggestions. Set up your people to shine by giving them room to process the issue on the way to an answer, and give them credit when they come up with a good solution.

Monitor yourself when you are in groups so you can become aware of any tendency you have to dominate the conversation. Sometimes you need to be out front and lead, but that's different from dominating and taking up all the air in the room.

Practice delegation, even if it makes you uncomfortable. Delegate and verify, but don't jump into the middle of what you delegated and hijack it back unless the consequences of not doing so would be dire.

Allow a little failure. We are all imperfect, and we all need a little failure to teach us how to succeed. To be clear, I'm speaking of a *little* failure here—the occasional mistake—not consistent failure as a way of life. We need to be human and allow for less than perfection for three reasons:

1. Perfection is not possible, so we are setting ourselves up for certain failure if we demand it.

2. If we fear failure too much, we get so tight that we guarantee ourselves more failure because that tightness degrades performance.

3. We learn many necessary and good lessons from failure. We only put our hands on top of a hot stove once, and sometimes we need to know what happens when we do that.

Be kind, no matter what. Kindness—treating people with consideration and respect—is a great builder of trust and good outcomes. Kindness does not take away the point you're trying to make; it allows people to relax enough to really get it. Sarcasm, browbeating, yelling, and or getting into people's physical space are no-nos.

Be fair. Don't manipulate people to get your way or gain advantage. Give everyone opportunities to succeed every day. That's your job, because when they succeed, you succeed.

Work with a mentor or coach for feedback and guidance about making these changes. No matter how smart we are, two heads are usually better than one, it's hard to see ourselves accurately in this regard, and old habits are hard to change.

TAKE ACTION FOR TRACTION:

One thing that I can do to only control what I really need to is: __

_____

_____

_____

Another thing I will look into that might help me take action on this is: _____

_____

_____

People and resources I might need to make this happen are: ____

_____

_____

_____

I will take action by this date: _____

CHAPTER 14

HOW TO FREE YOURSELF FROM YOUR FRUSTRATIONS

Frustrations and limitations of working at a job, please let me introduce you to the frustrations and limitations of self-employment. Doing the same job every day for the same grouchy boss in

> **ANOTHER REASON PEOPLE BECOME ENTREPENEURS:**
>
> **ENTREPRENEURS HAVE HAD IT WITH THE DAILY FRUSTRATIONS AND LIMITATIONS OF EMPLOYMENT.**

the same dysfunctional office can definitely make you want to chew your leg off to get out of the trap. But as you now know, frustrations and limitations on an even bigger scale come with running your own business.

Cliques and feuds may infest your worker relationships. You can't do all the work that comes your way in a day because you don't have the people or infrastructure in place for it. Someone critical to your business leaves. Your people need solid, long-term management, but you haven't developed internal leaders yet, and good leaders are not easy to find externally.

One of the hardest parts of business growth is that the entrepreneur owner's job description is always changing. Last year you were focused on getting the right people, and this year you've shifted to ramping up sales. As you increase your business size, your job shifts, too, and becomes more about managing your managers than managing your workers directly. It's easy when your tasks change like this to slide from an area where you are operating out of your strengths into a place where what you're doing is not really your thing, but there you are anyway.

That's a recipe for frustration.

SCORING

Give yourself a score for how you are currently doing with the frustrations and limitations of your business, on a scale of 1 to 10. (1 is "My frustrations about my business are really getting in the way," and 10 is "The frustrations and limitations of my business are very manageable, and I am happy with how I'm doing in this area.")

Your score between 1 and 10 is _____.

THE FIX

You need a good job description update every year to keep bringing you back to your core work because there are many distractions, lots of constant activity, and a line of people wanting a piece of you. It's easy to go from fire to fire and forget why you are really there and what you really need to do.

Don't lose yourself. The biggest risk in owning a business is that you will lose yourself in it. Owning a business, especially one that is growing, can be like stepping into fast-moving water that sweeps you away every day. There is so much to do, so much your people want from you, and so many important decisions to be made that you can become too immersed and lose the big picture. You can also get so "big picture" that you lose the basic steps of doing your day—or you get into everyone else's business to the detriment of yours.

Address frustrations when they arise. It's easy to sweep frustrations under the rug, especially if other things in your life are going well. Profits are up, so working Saturdays isn't as onerous as it otherwise might be. You have a great personal assistant, except that she cracks her gum for an hour after every meal or snack. You get a big new contract, so it becomes easier to ignore a smaller customer you don't like.

The thing is, though, if you don't address frustrations when they come up, they'll grow up to be real problems, and then you'll have to deal with them in bigger, more expensive ways.

There's a bit of an art to addressing frustrations well.

1. *Allow yourself to feel frustrated.* Frustration, by the way, is the little cousin of anger. It's actually an irritation, so learn to be aware of any irritability that you feel in any repetitive or ongoing way.

2. *Name it.* What is it that frustrates you? Say it, write it down, and admit it. I know, that means you'll feel compelled to do

something about it, which has risks, but it's either that or the frustration will end up doing to your feelings what an untended sliver does to your finger.

3. *Strategize a solution.* When you finally feel a frustration you've been avoiding, the temptation is to charge right out there and do something about it. Taking time to think things through first can't hurt unless it helps you delay and sweep what you're frustrated about back under the rug, in which case, charging out there is better than stuffing the frustration again.

4. *Take care of yourself.* Business leadership includes a standing invitation to forget about yourself and your own needs. Doing this may feel heroic and right in a sense—giving your all for the goal—but the price of not taking care of yourself ultimately makes you a less effective leader, husband, wife, or friend.

Factors that will really cost you at work if you don't get enough include:

- Sleep
- Vacations
- Physical fitness
- Conferences and gatherings where you can recharge and learn in your field
- Family and friend time
- Do-nothing time

Knowing now, from experience, that you will always have frustrations, no matter where you are in the development of your company, it is clear that the only way through them is to meet them and overcome them in a savvy way. Avoidance is not a strategy, and storing up too many frustrations will go boom sooner or later.

TAKE ACTION FOR TRACTION:

One thing I can do right away to reduce frustrations at work is: __

_____

_____

Another thing I will look into that might help me take action on this is: _____

_____

People and resources I might need to make this happen are:_____

_____

_____

I will take action by this date: _____

CHAPTER 15

THE RAT RACE IS NOT FOR YOU

> **ANOTHER REASON PEOPLE BECOME ENTREPENEURS:**
>
> **ENTREPRENEURS WANT TO GET OUT OF THE RAT RACE.**

Rats are fiercely competitive; they will fight over food and just about everything else.

> "Rat race: A way of life in which people are caught up in a fiercely competitive struggle for wealth or power... an exhausting, usually competitive routine."
> —Google Dictionary

When people speak of wishing to get out of the rat race, they are usually referring to having very demanding or boring jobs that they would like to leave behind. Even more, there is a desire in that phrase to get out of the whole *world* of people going to and fro every day to spend their time in other people's offices in demanding or boring jobs.

Some people, when they feel this way, dream of being entrepreneurs, and in those dreams they are happy because their work is exciting, meaningful, and interesting, and the people at work are great to be around. And, they won't have to ride the train with strangers falling asleep on their shoulders anymore.

They want to get out of their current work lives and into better ones.

There's nothing wrong with that, and a lot of entrepreneurs are born this way—they summon their considerable courage and find a way out of the rat race and into owning their own businesses.

At this point, a little discussion about the word *honeymoon* might be in order.

When we get fed up with anything—a job, a career, or a relationship—we move on to something that feels new and better sooner or later. Once we do that, we tend to fall in love with our new venture. We feel passionate about our new work every day, along with a great release of pent-up energy and a joyfulness about turning the page.

Whether you got to entrepreneurship by escaping a rat race or you just went for your dream, this place of beginnings is the honeymoon phase of your new business.

Just as with all honeymoons, it is a period of loving and bonding—nature's way of strongly connecting us with the people and things we love so we won't flee when hard times show up later.

Honeymoons end, but that's not a bad thing.

Stuff comes up, difficulties arise here and there, and managing people is absolutely the hardest part of running a business. At some point in any relationship, the truth of the relationship is revealed—that it is a mixture of good and bad, happiness and challenges. This is as true about your relationship with your business as it is about your relationship with your spouse.

Hopefully there is enough good and enough happiness in your relationship with your business that taking on the challenges that come with it is an acceptable part of the deal that won't destroy your happiness. In a good relationship, challenges give you lots of opportunities to grow, which result in greater happiness once you successfully navigate them.

If you successfully negotiated the honeymoon phase of owning your business and are well along the road of healthy business development, it is still quite possible that periods of challenge can come along that are big enough to make you feel as though you're back in a rat race again. You're exhausted, things aren't working right, people are being difficult. Whatever the reasons, you're grinding it out again.

If you know a couple who have been together for a long time, at some point you will hear them say something like, "Remember back in 2010, how we didn't get along well for almost a year?" Periods of hardship are inevitable and normal in every part of our lives, and they happen in business, too. When they come to you in your business from time to time and you start feeling as though you're in a rat race again, the challenge also brings an opportunity to assess what you're doing so you can recommit to better ways and to make other changes as necessary.

The restoration of your workplace happiness is important work. Allowing joyfulness to slip back into constantly grinding it out again is not an option.

SCORING

Give yourself a score for how much your work life feels like a rat race, on a scale of 1 to 10. (1 is "My work feels like a rat race, and I hate that feeling," and 10 is "I still really like having my own business, and I am happy with how I'm doing in this area.")

Your score between 1 and 10 is _____.

THE FIX

As the tasks of running a business keep getting more complex and demanding, perhaps you no longer have enough time or focus for what you are really passionate about. Your daily work may have shifted into areas that don't excite you, causing you to leave your passion behind.

This happened to me as a younger entrepreneur. I loved photography and was good at it, so I decided to open a professional photography studio. My thinking was that since I loved it so much, doing photography as a business would surely increase the love; I would be rolling in happiness like a horse in sweet clover.

There were two big flaws in that line of thinking.

First, once the actual photographing was surrounded by all the trappings of business, whatever joy there was tended to get lost in all that processing, mailing, office work, tax-paying, banking, and dealing with customers stuff.

Second, doing so much photographing all the time gradually overwhelmed my desire to take photos—even for pleasure—until I was no longer in touch with loving the photographic process. Turning it into a business had taken the joy out of it for me, and without joy my business had become one big chore.

I ultimately decided to close my photography business because it was unacceptable to me to lose my love of photography. There were lots of other things I could do for a living, and I wasn't about to give up taking beautiful photos. Fortunately, my love of photography as a hobby returned, and it remains one of my biggest joys to this day.

If you are in a situation where your love of what you do has gone low or missing, you are in danger of feeling as though you're back in the rat race. I'm not saying you should just shut down your business, though, because there are some things to think about first that might help you figure out what really needs to be done.

A passion for what you do isn't something you can just turn back on like a faucet. If you've noticed a decrease in your enjoyment of what you used to really love about your work, there are probably a number of issues to address before you're back in your passion again.

Could it be that you are burned out, that you've run yourself into the ground in some way to the point where you don't have any more juice to give to your business until you get a recharge? This happens a lot for entrepreneurs. Sometimes the people who care about us will spot this before we do. If there's been someone in your life saying, "You *really* need to take a break," maybe it's time to consider that.

Of course, for a break to work, it needs to be a real rejuvenation, not just a few days on the beach with your laptop and your phone turned on for business. Ideally, you go away and someone else runs the company for a while. Your computer is on only for the books you loaded into it, and your phone is on only so you can talk to the people who are dear to your personal life, and that's it.

You might find, though, that you're addicted to your work and can't disconnect, or that, for other reasons, you can't get away completely. If so, try taking some three-day weekends—some shorter breaks where you change the scenery and still get meaningful rest and renewal.

When you've had a break, start thinking about your business again—about what still engages you and what doesn't. Start imagining what it would be like for you to do more of what turns you on and less of whatever gets in the way.

If, for instance, you are a cook who started a restaurant and you don't get to cook much anymore, consider how you could prioritize doing more cooking and doing less of the business part. This could mean you hire some help with the business stuff, or you contract out whatever you can. Maybe changing your hours of operation or adjusting the size of your business to be larger or smaller would help.

You know the variables for your business—all the possibilities. Write them down and start shuffling them around until some new, better combination of factors snaps into place.

The rules for reimagining your business to bring the joy back into it are pretty simple:

- *All ideas are good*—you can reject or tweak them later. When your mind starts chattering at you that this or that won't work, gently go around that input and keep your creative mind open anyway, the way you would slow down your car to go around a rock in the road and then keep driving. Tell your mind, "Thank you for sharing," and then stay focused on the possibilities.

- *Keep a device or a pad of paper* with you at all times to record your spur-of-the-moment ideas—the good stuff that pops up when you're doing something else.

- *Use both the analytical and feeling parts of yourself* to keep checking out what you come up with. Don't over-think, and don't over-feel.

- *Test new ideas in a small way first* when you hit on something that you think is worth a try before going all in. Stick your toe in the water first.

This is also where neutral feedback and assistance from others can be very valuable. But bring other people into your evaluation only if you trust them completely to give you good, clean feedback and advice. Allow their points of view to show you possible opportunities for change and resolution, but beware of agendas they may have that are not congruent with yours. Create or revise your strategic plan, a succession plan, a selling plan—whatever plan or plans you need for operational guidance. Once you have completed those preparations, implement the changes you wish to make.

The bottom line here is to love what you do and love how you do it, and be vigilant about anything that would pull you away from those two things. As long as you are true to these core values, you will be free of the rat race.

TAKE ACTION FOR TRACTION:

One thing I can do right away to renew my passion for my work is: _____

_____

_____

Another thing I will look into that might help in this regard is:___

_____

_____

_____

People and resources I might need to make any of this happen are:

_____

_____

_____

I will take action by this date:_____

CHAPTER 16
BUSINESS FROM THE HEART

The latest yearly Gallup survey about the perceived honesty and ethics of business executives gives them an extremely low 17% "high" or "very high" score by the

ANOTHER REASON PEOPLE BECOME ENTREPENEURS:

ENTREPRENEURS WANT TO MAKE A POSITIVE DIFFERENCE IN THE WORLD.

public. This survey is about all top executives, not just business owners, and does not break out entrepreneurs as a distinct subset of those surveyed, which I think is a big mistake.

Entrepreneurial and big business values and behaviors often diverge widely.

A number of large business enterprises have decided in recent times that they have only one responsibility as a business, and that is to be profitable for their shareholders. That's it, and decisions made within those boardrooms on that basis are often made with only profits in mind.

Many large companies and most entrepreneurs do not share those values, but everyone gets tarred with the same brush in a survey when that's the behavior that makes headlines.

A high percentage of entrepreneurs I've known over the years have very strong values about wanting their companies to make a positive difference in the world. Not only do they hold those values personally, but most also incorporate them into the daily operation of their organizations. They do that through their vision and mission statements, ethics and accountability statements, initiatives and events, direct sponsorship, and financial support of community and worldwide organizations with similar values as well as through their relationships with their workers, customers, and vendors.

SCORING

Give yourself a score for your efforts to make a positive difference in the world, on a scale of 1 to 10. (1 is "I'd like to do more, but I haven't figured that one out yet," and 10 is "I am happy with how I'm doing in this area.")

Your score between 1 and 10 is _____.

THE FIX

When we want to make a positive difference in the world, the number one place to begin is to work from our hearts as well as our minds and to encourage others in our businesses to do the same.

Business has for ages been about setting aside feelings and working mostly from our thinking brains, and the loss of those feelings from the business mix has not helped our business worlds or the bigger world in which we live. It has been accepted as a given that we are supposed to leave our feeling, personal selves at home and bring only our mentally contained selves to work, and that is unrealistic at best. It is unhealthy and virtually impossible to shut down half of one's being all day to operate from the other half. That would be like only using your right arm and not using your left arm at all. We are meant to use all of ourselves—our talents, beliefs, values, thoughts, feelings, dreams, and desires—to live lives that matter and contribute to the common good.

When we get great new ideas, they usually don't come from our thinking process. They tend to pop up when we're not thinking—on a walk, awakening from sleep, or in the shower. They also tend to come to us about things we care about, things that involve our hearts—our feeling, sensing selves.

When great ideas pop up, they make us want to go share the news, and this excitement often brings on even more good ideas, more fun, and more excitement. Then our minds can get busy figuring out how to use them.

The mind and the heart are meant to be partners—onboard with each other, at work, and in the world.

So, working from the heart means that you bring your whole self to work, and you do your work from your thinking, feeling, sensing self, with all those parts of you contributing to your creativity and productivity.

As to specifically *how* you make a difference and contribute to the good in the world, your business influences the lives of everyone who comes in contact with it, and to care about that—to care about the people you touch, the people you employ, the customers who buy from you, and the community in which you operate, in addition to shareholder value—is a very good thing.

When you bring your heart to work with you, ways and means will come to mind about how you can actively make a positive difference in the world. You can enlist your people to come up with ways to do it, too. Giving yourselves to that purpose or project will be good for the world and good for your business.

When you bring all of you to work, you are much more likely to be a happy person, and your happiness will touch all those with whom you work. That's making a meaningful difference in the world in itself, and it should be a starting point for whatever externally focused efforts you decide to make to change the world for the better. When you consider the whole world, there's a big range of choices about how you can do that. If, as many others do, you want to support an organization that performs a great service, here are some things to consider when you are choosing your involvement.

What are your social values? Outdoor clothing maker Patagonia cares about the environment and donates 1% of its sales to environmental protection organizations around the world. It's a business no-brainer that Patagonia would support the environment where their products are used, but the people there are also working *in* the environment every day and see its needs, so they are personally motivated as well. If you decide to donate to a cause in some way, start by choosing an effort that aligns with your company *and* your personal values. If you are not clear about what your company values are, this is a good opportunity to figure them out. They should be strong, short, and clear—no jargon—and you want to include them as part of your company's vision or mission statement.

In addition to doing good things for the world, there are also marketing and tax advantages to supporting a charity. The searchable archive of the *New York Times* has a great article about how to wisely choose a charity.

You can also get reports about a charity you are considering from the Better Business Bureau.

TAKE ACTION FOR TRACTION:

One thing I can do right away to increase how I make a positive difference in the world is: _____

_____

_____

Another thing I will look into that I might do in this regard is: ___

_____

_____

People and resources I may need to make this happen are: _____

_____

_____

I will take action by this date: _____

The happiest entrepreneurs I know are those who have their hearts turned on along with their brains. They care about what they do, they care about their people and their workplaces, and they care about giving back.

As we conclude this section about you, the entrepreneur, and how you can have more happiness at work, it is easy to see how many demands are made on you as a business leader and how easy it can be for your happy self to sink out of sight and grow dim while your problems rise to dominate your attention.

Happiness requires attention and maintenance in order to last, and your well-being and happiness need to be on your radar just as strongly as your sales numbers and your employee retention rate. They need to be things you think about, measure, strategize about, and act on for long-term business and personal success. You can't have a workplace full of happy people unless you tend to your own happiness first because you can't lift someone else up if your own feet are not on solid ground.

So finding happiness at work, from an entrepreneur's standpoint, is about doing whatever is needed to revitalize your vision and your motivation—your business dream and your excitement—so you can wake up in the morning excited to go to work and be happy at work once you get there.

PART 4

Happy People to
Work for You

CHAPTER 17

SURVIVAL OF THE FITTEST: CHARLES DARWIN'S INFLUENCE ON AMERICAN BUSINESS

The brilliant scientist Charles Darwin published his theory of evolution in 1859. Its basic tenet was that the strongest survive through endless cutthroat competition and that the strong do (and should) crush the weak in that process.

Darwin became famous and immensely popular, and many American business barons of the day embraced this idea as a validation for their highly, umm… *competitive* business practices. This philosophy that competition is the most valid determiner of who survives and advances in business still holds sway in many enterprises large and small. It sets up a framework where business is viewed as a battle and where workers are soldiers who fight other businesses and each other to survive.

This is business as war.

In situations where someone else has lost out, someone in the work environment is likely to say, "It's not personal—it's just business." Business values in America have a history of being at least somewhat impersonal and opportunistic on the employer side of things, and that has been accepted as okay because Darwin said that's the way the world of nature is, and we're part of nature.

That hasn't been much fun for the workers who were caught up in this system, and trust between workers and employers has often been a casualty of this perspective, which by its nature sets everyone up to be adversaries.

So having happy employees may not be as easy or as straightforward as you would like, because there is a lot of painful history and habit in the background to overcome on both sides.

There is also another reason it's going to take some time and persistent effort on your part to create a happy workplace. One additional historical truth about the relationship between bosses and workers gets in the way big-time, and that is the inherent power imbalance in the relationship.

The boss has the money that the workers need for survival and thus usually has a greater degree of control in the owner/worker relationship. Of course, it is sometimes true that the balance shifts to where there aren't enough qualified workers to do the work, no matter how much money there is, which gives more power to the workers, but the more common relationship status has been boss-on-top, boss-in-charge, worker needs the boss more than the boss needs the worker, and workers are replaceable.

Before you can be a good boss who supports your workers' happiness, check out your inner Darwin—that place in you that believes workers are just there for your use and benefit in the business machine. Check yourself for those old attitudes and beliefs—places in you and ways of doing things where Darwin may still be at war with your new and better way.

Darwinian theory says: *In business, there are winners and losers, and competition is the best way to select winners and leaders. To the victors go the spoils.*

In order to have happy employees, you need to bring them home from this war. Some competition is good, but for it to work right, it needs to happen within a more collaborative overall environment where everyone's interests are viewed as equally important, and getting along and supporting each other's success are the norm. This is what your new young workers want because this culture is productive and feels good. A culture built purely on competition is toxic; for workers, it becomes all about winning and defending what's theirs from each other and from you.

When your people are happy, they'll make you happy. When they succeed, you succeed.

CHAPTER 18

WHAT MAKES YOUR PEOPLE HAPPY AT WORK?

As listed previously, the many benefits of having happy workers are huge, both for them and for you. Some of the biggest benefits for you are that your workers will be more engaged, do better work, get along better with coworkers, have fewer sick days and absences, and stick with you for the long haul.

So, what are the benefits of happiness at work for your people?

This is where we explore how you can make a major contribution to their happiness and why you should make the effort.

It all starts with you being genuinely interested in your workers and their well-being. This is an attitude on your part where their success matters as much to you as your own. Historically, although business owners have viewed workers as being necessary to the company's success, it was pretty much in a one-way, "what you can do for me" context. Workers only had value to a company for their contribution to its success, not necessarily to theirs as well. Workers, for their part, felt that their employment value was that of a tool, not a person.

For real workforce productivity and happiness, though, you need to care about more than just how they contribute to your own needs and success. As in any viable relationship, you need to care about others *as much as you care about yourself.*

The fact is, your real job is make your workers successful, to give them what they need to shine—n*ot just because you need them to produce for you,* but also because you care about them as human beings. When you support their success as workers *and* as people, they will give that level of support back to you; they will do great work, and when they are happy they will be a joy in your workplace and a boost to your bottom line.

In negotiations with workers about compensation, the conversation in previous times used to be mainly focused on pay and some rather standard company benefits—health insurance, time off, and sick days. That has all changed, and it's a good thing. More on why it's good in a moment.

Workers today want many things you may have never had because their priorities are different than yours were, depending upon your age difference.

Their first priority is to have a happy life overall, a life that isn't just centered around work. And when they do go to work, they want to be in happy environments where they can enjoy doing the work itself and where they can also enjoy the *experience* of the workplace. They want to do satisfying work in a good, human environment, and they will not stay with jobs that don't provide them with that experience.

American University recently released a report about what young people want in life. James C. Dinegar, president and chief executive officer of the Greater Washington Board of Trade, a sponsor of the study, said of today's market for workers, "If you're just a rank-and-file company with X number of days off and no flexibility, you can move to the back of the line. There are higher and different expectations now."

In America, many younger workers have known lives of relative abundance; most of them didn't worry about the next meal, and they had some money to buy things. They are moving up through Maslow's Hierarchy of Needs, from primary concerns about safety and security to being able to focus more on love and belonging, family, friendship, community, and a sense of connection. Self-esteem is important to them—the need to be and feel like a good and unique individual.

This is the natural progression for people in a society in which life improves from generation to generation. Once safety needs are met, other things start to matter more than just a paycheck (survival), and it's human nature to climb that Maslow's Hierarchy of Needs ladder.

It would be very helpful to your relationships with your workers if you could understand and allow for this progression and not just think of them as spoiled brats. What they want matters. It should matter, and it would have mattered to you, too, if you'd been fortunate enough to grow up at a later time in America when workplace priorities had become more balanced between work and human needs.

In the generations before the Baby Boomers, people were primarily concerned with having good, secure jobs that they could stay with for a long time. It was about doing whatever it took to land a job and make the boss happy, and that need was so primary—at the survival level in Maslow's hierarchy—that happiness was not a major factor. If you were happy, that was good, but you did whatever it took to get and keep the job, period. If the hours were long and you had to make your job the biggest part of your life, so be it. You were lucky to have that job.

It's easy to see how business owners from that time and that experience of work can feel envious, and perhaps even resentful, about the work values and priorities of young workers today.

But it is a *really good thing* that these young workers are helping us take our sour, dour Puritan past out of today's workplace. It's a grand thing to spend most of our waking hours in a place where the work is good and people are happy. And, it is so important to connect up who we are at work with who we are at home.

It's about time for us to be ourselves in both environments.

So, what makes your people happy at work? Here is what workers say when you ask them what matters most:

1. I love my work.
2. My purpose, goals, and aspirations are supported by working here.

3. I have good relationships and interactions with people at work.

4. I am treated with respect, fairness, and trust.

5. My job has some variety, challenges, and autonomy.

6. I am comfortable in my physical workspace.

7. I matter to this company, to my team, and to the larger work of the organization.

8. I am proud of my organization.

When workers experience these things, they have a sense of well-being—an underlying perception that the puzzle pieces of the world of work are snapping together and going well for them and that they are making a contribution. This in turn produces feelings of happiness, which might include joy, contentment, satisfaction, self-esteem, or delight. This list could—happily—be a long one.

So when I'm talking about happiness at work, that is shorthand for two different but connected things—a state of well-being, which includes a solid sense of rightness about the work aspect of a person's life, and the happy emotions that come with it.

It sounds quite technical to separate them this way, but the distinction is a very important one when we start thinking about how you can actively contribute to your workers' happiness. I am talking about how you can contribute to their actual well-being, from which happy feelings will naturally come.

Focus first on how to increase your workers' well-being because you will be increasing real value for them in their lives, and that is what creates lasting happiness. Use this as a lens when you are considering something you think might be good for them and ask yourself, "Is what I am thinking of doing going to contribute to real well-being for these people, or will it just be a 'feel-good' buzz that doesn't have any lasting meaning or depth?"

Since our culture usually defines happiness as a set of desirable emotions that are not necessarily attached to any bedrock sense of well-being, some leaders concentrate more on encouraging happy emotions for their people than on what would contribute to their deeper well-being.

Bringing in a chef to cook for them may impress, and workers may enjoy the result, but how deeply does this contribute to their foundational well-being?

Having a dog-friendly workplace may create a sense of well-being for some people, but for others who aren't dog people, probably not so much.

Offering generous vacation and leave time, on the other hand, has strong well-being potential for those who will use them. Being able to work at least part of the time from home is also an enhancement to well-being for workers who can function well in that setup. Bonuses and improved benefits score highly with workers across the board as meaningful contributions to their well-being.

Beyond those measures, companies are finding it somewhat difficult to come up with ways to enhance well-being across the board for everybody in an organization, so they are making piecemeal efforts toward it wherever they can. Sometimes those efforts produce real value—genuine well-being—and sometimes they miss the mark.

Leaders usually go for a piecemeal approach to things like this when they don't have a coherent strategy about it yet, so they start throwing things out there to see what sticks. The idea of companies taking action to focus on the happiness of their workers is great, but it is still pretty new, so they are in the experimental stage with their offerings.

Experimentation is necessary and good sometimes, but what we're going to do in the next section is to explore how you can provide eight very substantial benefits for your workers that influence their happiness the most. These are things that we know all workers want because they told us—no experimenting was needed.

If you do these things and make them the basis of your company culture for everyone, you will create a workplace environment that will encourage well-being and happiness for all your workers.

So here we go. Here's how you can support your people in being happy at work, point by point.

CHAPTER 19

I LOVE MY WORK

"You can only become truly accomplished at something you love. Don't make money your goal. Instead, pursue the things you love doing and then do them so well that people can't take their eyes off you."
—Maya Angelou

Loving one's work is the ideal motivation to create great work output and to have a good time doing it. In the ideal workplace, people love their work. I'm speaking of a solid love for the actual work that is performed, where people know that it is just the right thing for them to be doing and they enjoy it. When people have that, they have a coming-home kind of feeling about their work.

When people love their work in this way, they are performing it from deep strength, and it shows. We all do best at what we love to do, so a worker who loves his or her work and can do that work for you and get paid for it is already set up for happiness. And, you are set up to have an ongoing pipeline of great work product from this person.

What can you do to create and encourage this love of work with the people you already have? What can you do to find more people like that?

THE FIX

Make a total commitment to have an "I love my work" company.

It isn't easy to do this, because a lot of reasons will surface down the line to weasel out of your commitment that will seem utterly compelling to you at the time.

Someone leaves or is let go, for example, and there's a big hole that must be urgently filled. The temptation to hire someone who can just do the work, never mind whether he or she loves it or not, can be very strong.

The long-term solution here is to *have depth at every critical position,* but in the meantime, bringing on a qualified temp or using a cross-trained backup worker temporarily could buy you time to find the right person for the job.

Use a recruiter to augment your own hiring resources. Yes, I know it's expensive, but recruiters have access to a lot of qualified candidates right now, and bringing in someone for the position who doesn't love it but who just shows up for the paycheck will cost you a lot more on many levels over time than the recruiter would.

You want your company to excel, right? You want to be the best? The best are deeply committed to staying the course with what they know to be right, no matter what. Commitment does interesting things to the mind. When people are totally committed to something, their minds stay focused and they open up to more solutions and creative ideas about the situation. Then life just seems to bring them more options and possibilities.

Identify and keep the workers you currently have who really love what they do. In a small company, you probably already know who they are; in a larger company, you can survey your supervisors and workers to find out. There are various assessment tools you can use to measure worker engagement at all levels. Retaining your happy people should be a very high priority. Turnover is expensive in so many ways, and losing your best performers is even worse.

Nic Marks, creator of the award-winning *Happy Planet Index* and the English firm *Happiness Works* has this to say about today's worker retention competition:

> "Nearly half of all employees plan to look for a new job in the next year. However, the issue becomes even more acute when you look at truly booming areas like the West Coast tech scene, for example. Not only are employment options vast for candidates in these high-growth industries, but also the know-how and expertise that they have acquired within their roles is extremely valuable, and the currency that those individuals hold becomes extremely high.

> "You can attempt to spend your way out of this conundrum, giving ever-more expansive pay raises and undertaking constant recruitment drives. However, there's a much simpler solution. The fact is, people who are happy in their jobs stay in their jobs. So, working on happiness and well-being in the workplace becomes the critical strategy to tackling talent retention."

Start building love of work into every position you have whenever there is an opening. Or, create an opening if you have someone there now who doesn't contribute some love to it and never will.

"Loves his or her work" needs to be a prominent, deal-breaker qualification for candidates who come to you for positions, and that means every position, from janitor to... you. Outside of possessing the proper skills to actually do the work, this is the most important qualification of all, so your job interviews need to include a prominent and thorough section about this, not just a rushed question or two. It is also an area that needs to be a strong focus when you contact a candidate's references.

You can get some of the information you need about whether your applicants are a good fit in this way by asking the following types of questions in your job interview:

- Tell me how you came to do this work.
- How do you feel about your work? On a scale of 1 to 10, how happy are you when you do your work?
- Tell me a little about your work process—how do you do what you do?
- Have you been acknowledged and appreciated for the quality of your work in the past, and if so, how?
- What do you see as your bright future for your work, and what's your plan to get there?

It's a good idea to add the Gallup Clifton StrengthsFinder assessment to any other skills assessments you use with candidates so you can find out how a person's complete range of strengths line up and whether those particular strengths are a good overall fit for the position. The Gallup assessment is extremely useful because it shows you not only what people's strengths are but also where the gaps are—what it will look like if you bring on someone who lacks a particular strength that is needed for the position. One of the most common money-sucking and time-wasting problems in entrepreneurial businesses is the assignment of work to people who are not well matched for it.

ASSETS	LIABILITIES
You love your work. You know that if you don't love your work, you won't insist that your people love theirs. Then nobody will be really happy, and you'll all be just okay, and you will have a just okay company.	You enjoy some parts of your work, and that's good enough. Life gives you the bad with the good.
You only hire people who love their work. It doesn't need to be love that's a ten on a ten-point scale, but they have to really, really like it a lot—at least nine-ish.	You believe that it is unreasonable to expect that everyone in a company will love their work. If they just stick around and do what they are paid to do, that's enough.
You know that love of work and the enjoyment of doing that work in your workplace are the keys to worker retention, so you measure these things and concentrate heavily on improving them for your people.	You believe that money talks and that more money will keep workers with you. Your worker incentives are mostly financial.

CHAPTER 20

MY PURPOSE, GOALS, AND ASPIRATIONS ARE SUPPORTED BY WORKING HERE

It used to be that work was work and personal life was personal, and never the twain would meet, but young workers today are determined that their work and personal lives support each other. They don't want to put on a different personality to go to work, and they aren't willing to be as work-centered as previous generations. They put a high priority on having time for a good life outside of work.

They are also likely to have a well-developed set of values, goals, and desires.

When they think about their life purpose, it often relates to making a difference in the world. They have seen the new transaction-based business world for what it is—how cold and lacking in loyalty and personal values it can be—so they view work as a means to an end, a way to fulfill their personal purpose and their personal goals.

In their way of looking at it, life comes first, and work comes second.

These new workers aren't willing to suffer much to get their needs met, either. They expect the workplace to feel good and to support them in authentically engaging with the people and tasks there. They want their work life to have meaning and be fun and interesting, and they want to be happy.

When you read this, it might seem that it's all about them and their needs, and you might worry that they won't fit in and may not give you the value you pay them for.

Your concerns are understandable, and some workers in every generation bring with them an oversized sense of entitlement that is unrealistic and off-putting, but these young workers on the whole can be very good for you—and very loyal—if you know how to work with them.

What makes them different?

They grew up in households where it was likely that both parents worked, so they learned to take care of themselves at an early age. They were "latch-key kids" who were home alone a lot, and computers became their companions and tutors. They played games, communicated with other kids, developed an online social life, and had a window on the world where anything and everybody was accessible instantly in real time.

They learned about instant gratification on computers—that they could change the scene with the click of a mouse.

Not feeling happy today? Click up a virtual party, buy some shoes, chat with friends about it. Largely because of computers, they grew up believing that they could change the world and change their version of the world instantly, whenever they wanted to.

We grew up navigating our neighborhoods; they grew up navigating the world.

So when it comes to work, consider how their viewpoint has evolved from yours. They are totally used to communication, they want it to be direct and immediate, and they don't like delays between knowing what they want to do and taking action on it. They are sometimes seen as arrogant, but some of that is just because they have experienced a (computerized) world where change is easy and you can have what you want with the click of a mouse. It is often a shock for them to find out that the workplace is not like that, but you, their leader, must consider whether they might have a point or three. Would your workplace be better if it were less complicated, if communication were better, and if changes could be made more easily?

Maybe you want some of the same things they want?

To succeed with these workers, you, the entrepreneur owner, must be able to support them in their worthy needs and in some of their different ways of doing things, and they will give you performance and loyalty in return. You must be able to support the achievement of both their work and their life goals, and you must do what you have to do to make your workplace a good and happy place for them. If you do those things, they will stay and do good work for you.

To expect them to put work first, though—to expect that they will give you long-term loyalty just for money, or to expect them to see you as The Boss to whom they must bow—is unrealistic. They see themselves as equal to you and your needs, and that's the way they want to be treated.

Wrap your head around that and back it up with action, and you'll do fine. The question is, what does the action part look like?

THE FIX

The biggest key to doing well with younger workers is, in one word, *communication.* They have grown up in a world full of constant, instant communication, and they are pretty good at it. They expect you to communicate clearly with them and for you to encourage and value their communication with you.

They want uncomplicated access to you, or to whoever manages them, so this two-way communication can occur quickly and easily. They do not like to work in businesses with a lot of management that slows things down. They want to talk to their boss directly and do not want policies and procedures getting in the way of the information they need.

For these reasons, they work best in flatter company structures where access to what they need in their work is easy and where collaboration within and between teams is the rule. They don't do as well in the full-on traditional vertical command-and-control structure where they have to jump through hoops to gain access to what they need in their work and where looking out for one's own advancement to the detriment of the team is the rule.

These young workers want transformative leaders—leaders who can motivate them, sound the call, and clearly communicate the purpose of their work, the company, and the future. They want you to define the purpose and challenge them to accomplish it with you. Motivation really counts for them!

They want to learn, and they want to understand their work, but the old ways of teaching aren't so effective. Mentoring and classes work best, along with an online training component. They also like to learn by observing, so assigning them to shadow people who do what you are trying to teach them to do is effective.

There is a fairly common belief that young workers are not loyal, but if they can build real relationships with you—not just receive your pearls of wisdom and instructions—they can be very loyal. Relationships matter to them, and they respond well to personalized advice and development.

They want accountability to run both ways, and mutual honesty is a must. You'd better walk your talk and be straight with them, or they'll be gone.

They work best when they have a simple management structure to work with—ideally a single manager. They want information and guidance when they want it, without having to deal with the complexity and politics of multiple managers.

Got all of that?

These young workers aren't necessarily narcissistic; they just grew up in a very different world than you did, and they have different, more direct ways of doing things. The new ways of the young generation are bumping up against the set ways of an older generation—a common dance through the ages.

ASSETS	LIABILITIES
You know that people aren't just working for a paycheck anymore and that they also want to enjoy the experience of working for you. You pay as much attention to whether they enjoy their work as you do to the work they perform for you.	Work is work, and it wasn't meant to be fun. You expect your people to come in and give you a fair day's work for a fair day's pay. They can have fun on their own time.
You are aware that many of your workers now work to live—they don't live to work. You have policies and initiatives in place that help them have a good life outside of work that matches up well with their work.	You give a week more of vacation time now than you did, and you give some sick days, too, even though you're not required to. Sometimes you have a barbecue after work or you all meet for drinks downtown, and the tab is on you.

ASSETS, CONT.	LIABILITIES, CONT.
You have invited young workers to interact with or participate on your executive team so they can represent the interests and desires of their peers. In this role, they help shape the company for their future as well as yours.	When these young workers prove that they can be responsible and settle down, you will promote them. They need to prove themselves to participate at a high level.
Yours is a company of communicators because you know that good communication is the foundation of all good things. You hire for it, you teach it, you model it, and you require it.	You just look for people who can do the work—no muss, no fuss. Your managers need to be able to get their point across, but everyone else just needs to do what they are directed to do.

CHAPTER 21

I HAVE GOOD RELATIONSHIPS AND INTERACTIONS WITH PEOPLE AT WORK

The biggest single historical factor that affects worker satisfaction is not money—it's relationships. Getting along well with the people they work with allows workers to tolerate a lot of other things that might be less than optimal. But if work relationships aren't good, everything else about the job is negatively affected, and the odds are much higher that your workers will seek new employment. Young workers in particular are very big on good communication and lots of it, and they want a healthy, happy work environment. They thrive on relationships and information, so if those are impaired in your workplace, they will move on.

Conflict and turmoil can cause damage to every part of a company if they are not dealt with quickly. Cliques form and departments silo up, sharply reducing collaboration and cooperation with each other. Things got so bad at one company I consulted with that conflicts and a lack of communication caused people in two departments not to communicate with each other at all about a critical production error that ultimately cost their company millions of dollars, a lost contract, and a damaged reputation.

One of the biggest problems in the workplace is that business leaders are sometimes really good at business and not so good with people. Yet if there are problems with your people, your business can be ruined.

What causes relationship issues at work?

When I lead trainings about conflict, I often start by asking everyone in the hall to please raise a hand if they've had good conflict-resolving role models at home. Not many hands go up.

From a psychological point of view, workplace conflicts are usually some form of reenactment of dramas from roles that people had at home. Bullies, tattletales, abusers, slackers, and enablers all have lengthy in-home training in those roles. We learn from our childhood caregivers how to do our relationships, and then we take that "training" into the workplace and act it out. The home is our relationship school, and unfortunately for many of us, it is the school of bad relationships. Not all families are dysfunctional, of course, and not all of your people become problems, but enough do that huge amounts of time and money are wasted because of issues with them at work.

When you decided to open your own business—a business that requires having people work for you—it probably only hit you later that the people part was going to be the biggest challenge to your success.

Out of our eight practices that make workers happy, good relationships at work come in at number one. They are the biggest weight on the scale, so figure this one out and you've got room for further development with some of the others.

THE FIX

Start by improving your hiring process. HR can definitely help with screening in very specific ways if you have an internal HR department. They probably already administer some assessments during the hiring process, so they can add measurement of each applicant's emotional intelligence—how he or she gets along with others at work—along with the Gallup's Clifton StrengthsFinder. I like the BarOn Emotional Quotient Inventory (EQ-i) assessment for this purpose.

The Myers-Briggs Type Indicator is also a good assessment, and many of the other DISC-type assessments out there are based at least somewhat on the MBTI. This assessment has been around for a long time and is a trusted resource.

Assessments are not perfect, but they give you some useful insights and clues about the people you are looking at for key positions before you have to make any major commitments to them.

I am not an HR expert, but here's part of what I see the HR pros doing in their companies' hiring process that makes sense to me:

- An initial screening interview with candidates over the phone to weed out obvious mismatches for the position.
- A first in-person interview that can be scored. Two of the biggest things you can do to improve your interviewing are to make all

interview questions the same for each position and to score your interviews. This will help reduce "intuitive hiring," where you hire applicants based on just getting a feeling that they are fine after you ask some non-standardized questions.

- A second in-person interview to ask more about whatever the first interview turned up and whatever you thought of after the person left.

- A peer interview—with standardized and nonstandardized questions—where the people whom the applicants would work with in your company get a chance to meet candidates and give you their impressions and recommendations. Involving your people in the interview process gives them a trusted role to play in your selection process, and it gives you a different and valuable perspective about your candidates.

- A very thorough set of reference checks. Dig deep, call everyone, and learn everything you can.

- A background check. These are easily purchased, and it's worthwhile to know whether your candidates are bringing big, hidden problems in your door.

If you do not have an HR department in-house, plenty of independent HR companies out there will be happy to provide you with hiring services on a menu or package basis. Yes, they cost money, but they can help you hire better people and keep out the bad apples, so it's worth every penny. They also reduce your legal exposure by setting up legally compliant processes for you regarding your other employment practices.

Get some outside help for conflicts. If you have conflicts in your workplace that resist resolution, it's time to get some help. Everyone hates conflict, and not many people know what to do about it.

What's most important about conflicts is that they need to be resolved as quickly as possible—before they can create lasting harm. If you hear of a conflict in your organization, bring in the supervisors of the parties involved and talk to them about it. Ask what they are doing or have done to resolve the issue, and if the answers don't sound realistic or aren't working, get some help with the situation pronto. If conflict goes on too long, it will traumatize your workers and create a toxic workplace, and there goes their happiness (and yours).

Teach your people how to communicate. Given that most people don't have good communication skills modeled for them in their early years, training your people how to be good communicators is a proactive step to take. It's always easier to prevent communication problems than to fix them after they've gotten a head start.

You can find a great number of online training resources on the topic of communication if you Google "online communication training." If you want a top-level class for your people, many universities are now streaming MOOC (Massive Open Online Course) classes for free.

If you have a university business school nearby, they may be able to refer you to good training resources.

There is also a book I highly recommend: *Crucial Conversations: Tools for Talking When Stakes Are High,* by Kerry Patterson.

ASSETS	LIABILITIES
When there is a conflict in your workplace, you pull it into supervision, either with a manager or with you. The appropriate person in the chain of command talks to the people involved, and if the situation remains unresolved, HR or a conflict management specialist gets involved. Conflicts are not allowed to simmer without intervention.	Sometimes you handle a conflict directly, without involving the supervisor of the people involved. You call them in and hear their stories, and if it's not an easy fix on the spot, you tell them to work it out "or else." If the conflict still doesn't resolve, you decide who the troublemaker is and take strong action to end the problem.
You evaluate all job applicants for their ability to work well with others. New hires are closely observed during a probation period to see, among other things, how good they are with people. You do not hire people, or allow people to stay, if they cannot get along well with others.	Getting the job done is the number one priority. If there's any trouble, you can put a stop to it.

ASSETS, CONT.	LIABILITIES, CONT.
You have a standardized hiring process that includes people other than yourself when making decisions about candidates. Interviews are scored, and criteria for hiring are clear and consistently applied.	You have a "boss's interview" with all candidates. You ask questions from a list you drew up, spend some time together, and if everything feels good by the end of the interview, you go ahead and hire.

CHAPTER 22

I AM TREATED WITH RESPECT, FAIRNESS, AND TRUST

These three attributes and their corresponding actions are keys to self-esteem and job performance. Self-esteem is about having reality-based confidence in our own worth and abilities. We all need a healthy sense of self-esteem to relate well with others and feel as though we deserve good things in life. People with low self-esteem aren't capable of feeling very happy, and they usually have poor self-esteem because they were not treated with enough respect, fairness, or trust somewhere along the way.

Self-esteem is not to be confused with narcissism, a word that originated with the god Narcissus in Greek mythology, a god who fell in love with his own image reflected in a pool of water. Narcissism is unhealthy self-esteem that is characterized by excessive self-approval and a strong sense of entitlement, often acted out at the expense of others. It is classified in psychiatry as a personality disorder.

Respect, fairness, and trust are essential cornerstones to treating your people well and developing good, trusting relationships with them. These three are critical for great work performance, and they must be operational to some degree in a person in order for that person to be truly happy.

Respect has several aspects: it is a feeling of deep admiration for someone elicited by their abilities, qualities, or achievements—"I really respect your honesty"—and it is also about having proper regard for the feelings, wishes, rights, and traditions of others—"I respect the differences in how we practice our religions."

When we are young, we need to experience a lot of respect to set up a foundation for future healthy relationships: "This is your room, and we won't come in without knocking" or "I really respect you for being truthful—for not lying to me." The first kind of respect in this example is about respecting boundaries—that we have a right to them and that they will be respected. The second kind of respect is about directly acknowledging to us the good in us, the best of who we are as people—truthful, giving, kind, and other things of that nature.

Having regular real-life demonstrations and feedback regarding these kinds of respect from our caregivers allows us to develop respect for others. We know what respect is because we receive it, and we can then turn around and give it to others. If we don't receive respect when we're young, we won't really know what it is or how to give it later on, and there will be a gap in our ability to treat people right.

THE FIX

This tendency toward lack of respect is a difficult deficit to correct, but people generally want to know how to get things right and succeed. If you use situations where they fail to show respect as teaching and learning opportunities, your respectful intervention to teach what respect looks like can be a corrective experience for the offender. This teaching-how-it-should-be approach is probably your best shot at creating a change in this type of undesirable behavior.

At work, people who lack a sense of respect may be negative and unforgiving toward others. They may be aggressive or have difficulty honoring necessary boundaries, and they may not know how to compliment people or acknowledge them for what they do right. Here's what you can do:

Contain them. Set limits and boundaries for them. "Please do not come into my office when I am with someone else or when the door is closed." "I would like you to get with HR to take an online course about respectful communication." When you observe or receive reports of disrespectful behavior, tell the person that the behavior is unacceptable, and also tell him or her what behavior would have been acceptable in those circumstances.

Start all your meetings at every level with "appreciations"—accolades for people who do good things. Be a model for acknowledgment of what is right and good. It's never too late to learn about respect.

Be fair to everyone. Fairness is about having some standards and rules, and sticking to them for everyone, but it is about more than that. Fairness is also a practice that comes from having respect for the people involved and for the organization or group rules. Fairness is when I know you will treat me just like the next person—that I, along with everybody else, will have my shot at good things.

A person who isn't fair usually has problems with respect, too.

Fairness starts with you. As the company leader, you must be impeccably fair. Leading without favor is absolutely necessary, or your organization will follow your bad example in this regard and trust will be hard to find anywhere. Unfairness as a business practice destroys trust and foments dishonesty.

1. Review policies and procedures with your leaders to be sure they are fair and just. Be sure that the system is not institutionalizing a lack of fairness in any area.

2. If you become aware of any of your people being unfair to their people, mentor them in this area until they change their behavior or let them go if they can't do that. Nothing destroys trust faster than a lack of fairness.

Trust is firm belief in the reliability, truth, ability, or strength of someone. "I trust you to always do the right thing" or "Even when I'm not around, I trust you to show up and do your job." Trust is a belief in the best in others. It often elicits that level of behavior in return when you give it because living up to someone's trust feels good. If our trust in someone is violated, we will usually revert to a more cautious evaluation of what to expect from that person from then on. "You're due in at 3:00. I'll call then to make sure everything is okay."

If you violate someone's trust, you can sometimes earn it back by being unrelentingly trustworthy in all you say and do from that time forward, but the road to forgiveness gets a lot tougher if you break trust again.

What is at the bottom of problems with trust?

Put simply, we lose our trust in people or institutions if they don't keep their word—if they don't deliver on explicit or implied commitments.

Your warehouse manager is supposed to do a certain piece of work for you and doesn't show up. A vendor says he'll get you what you need in three days and it takes seven. Your VP says she will have paperwork for you by Friday, but it floats onto your desk the following Tuesday.

The first time these kinds of things happen with someone, don't let them slide, because you need to find out if it was a one-time slip and you really can trust them or if it was one of a series of actions of an untrustworthy person. The person also needs to know that your trust was broken, and you need to put him or her on notice about it.

"When we had an agreement to meet at the warehouse Tuesday at 3:00 and you didn't show up, I felt (name feelings: confused, mad, sad, and so on), and I need to know why you didn't keep the appointment. Also, if we make another appointment and you don't make it, you will damage my trust in you, and there will be these consequences (name consequences)."

Trust can often be healed if there is a one-time occurrence that is not repeated. We all make mistakes, but multiple trust-breaking actions usually damage the relationship, and you are then left to decide what action to take about this untrustworthy person.

Respect, fairness, and trust must be in place for you and your people before you can all be happy at work. Levels of each of those things don't have to be perfect—people aren't perfect—but the overall sense must be that this is a respectful, fair, and trustworthy workplace.

ASSETS	LIABILITIES
You know that one of your tasks as company leader is to actively monitor what goes on in your workplace regarding fairness. You take proactive and transparent corrective action whenever you see unfairness happening anywhere.	If someone comes to you with an issue of fairness, you deal with it behind closed doors.
You provide online or in-person training to your people about how to communicate respectfully. You enforce respectful communication in all conversations that you observe and in which you have a part.	Sometimes you yell at one of your people, or you swear when you're upset. A little sarcasm in a meeting doesn't hurt anything, either. People need to be able to vent.
Your word is your bond. If you say you're going to do something, you do it, and you do it at the promised time.	You try to keep your word, but sometimes things get so hectic that you forget about a commitment or you have to put it off until you can get to it.

CHAPTER 23

MY JOB HAS VARIETY, CHALLENGES, AND AUTONOMY

Some jobs have built-in variety, challenges, and autonomy, and others don't. If you're a salesman, every day is full of a wide variety of people and tasks, every sale is a challenge, and you may have some autonomy about how you close a sale. If you are a factory assembly-line worker, you might have limited variety, challenges, and autonomy.

This doesn't mean that the salesman isn't bored with his work in his larger sphere of freedom or that the assembly-line worker is dissatisfied with the precise and repetitive nature of her job. But if your people do any collection of tasks over and over again, whether it's selling or assembly-line work, the endless familiarity of the work can sometimes get to them and diminish their engagement and happiness.

Fortunately, there are things you can do, some small and others that are more substantial, to tweak the situation so the person is more engaged again.

THE FIX

Most of us are born with an urge to advance, to move forward in life. Just watch the impatience of drivers in a line of cars when the light turns green.

But.

When it comes to a job, some workers want to advance, and they enjoy change, but for others the unchanging routine of the job where they are is just what they like. They are reassured by it and react badly to changes. It is good to be aware that you probably have workers with both inclinations, and you might want to be aware of who likes what in this regard before you start changing routines. One size of change management does not fit all.

What this means in practical terms is that it's a good thing to approach change in the workplace with a well-thought-out plan that takes these differences into account, and any change you contemplate should be thoroughly communicated to your workers before, during, and after its implementation.

That said, here are three basic ways to enhance variety, autonomy, and healthy challenges for your workers once they are properly prepared for them:

1. Evaluate the specific work in detail, with an eye toward increasing the worker's large- or small-scale decision-making. The salesman might be encouraged to make more autonomous decisions about finding and approaching new prospects. The assembly worker might be given an additional role in evaluating her part of the assembly process and making recommendations for assembly and safety changes she thinks are needed.

2. Look for new skills that workers can learn that would expand or enhance the scope of their work. An advertising artist-illustrator can start contributing illustrations for books as well as ads. A meteorologist (weather forecaster) can learn how to deliver forecasts on a radio weather broadcast in addition to assembling them.

3. Increase the impact of a worker's job. Widen the shift supervisor's reporting function to include the operations manager as well as his unit manager. Choose a socially adept worker to represent the company at an ongoing networking meeting.

In these examples, specific changes are made to the responsibilities of the workers, even in very small ways, that help them increase their competence and gain a greater sense of well-being and happiness.

Raises and promotions are traditional ways to do that, but it's more long-lasting to give your workers a sense of forward movement and advancement in other ways, too. It isn't necessarily the size or type of advancement that matters but rather the sense of forward motion itself.

ASSETS	LIABILITIES
You know who thrives on forward movement and who wants to feel secure with things as they are, and you tailor your approach to changes with them accordingly.	You have a baseline expectation that workers will stay engaged for the paycheck and that they will accept whatever changes you make because they are necessary.
You know when your workers get bored and need some changes because you are attuned to their moods and needs. They might even trust you enough to tell you about it.	When people get bored, they act out in all kinds of ways instead of just saying, "I'm bored." If you don't know the difference, you'll spend a lot of time putting out fires instead of recalibrating their work responsibilities and routines to get them interested again.
You coach your people through change instead of just dumping it on them.	You initiate too much change too fast and expect your people to just get with the program.

CHAPTER 24

I AM COMFORTABLE IN MY PHYSICAL WORKSPACE

You don't have to be in a modern suite of offices with lots of room for each person's workspace, but the workplace you are in must meet some standards, or the lack of them will make your people unhappy.

I have a coaching client who owns a service company he started himself. Looking for space, he initially had to settle for an old office building with small rooms, green walls, bad fluorescent lighting, and worn brown carpet. His personal office had a radiator that clanked and groaned whenever it came on, and the conference room barely accommodated a scarred table and half a dozen chairs. It was what he could afford at the time.

Eventually the company did well and his staff grew. He's a pretty thrifty guy, though, so he viewed his now-crowded funky offices as a big cost saving, and he didn't upgrade to a new place for years. People jammed into the conference room for weekly sales meetings, always standing room only, with overflow in the hallway. People in the accounting department worked shoulder to shoulder, six in a room made for three.

The work got done, and because he was an otherwise good leader, the workers endured the space. They tuned it out and forged ahead. It wasn't a happy place, but the work got done.

Finally he realized that the so-so surroundings could be hurting his bottom line. As his business grew, he began to meet with very substantial people who wanted to transact very big deals with him, and he suddenly realized that to invite these people into this old, cramped, and ugly space was not a good thing. It was incongruent with his stature and reputation and with the image he needed to project to create trust at this level, and that could cost him sales.

He moved his company to a new, roomy, light-filled downtown building six months later. Everyone walked around stunned at first, some people literally with their mouths open. One employee was heard to say, "I think I just got out of jail."

When I talked to him after a few months had passed, he said, "You wouldn't believe how things have changed. Everybody walks around smiling with a spring in their step, and new business is just pouring in. I know I was afraid of the costs of this move, but it's the best thing I ever did for my business—and for my people."

Another client is a real estate agent and a very good one. He worked for a brokerage and consistently outsold all the other agents there, but his goal was to become a millionaire and his growth had flattened out. He called one day and asked if I would help him brainstorm about it.

I asked him about his work, who his customers were, and how he became so successful. Nothing stood out in his answers as a cause for the invisible ceiling on his income.

Then I asked where he worked, and here came the answer we were looking for.

It turns out that he worked most of the time at his home, in a partly finished basement office at a "desk" made of a large door resting on file cabinets. There were no windows and only a few utilitarian lights. He didn't see clients there, but it's where he spent most of his time when he wasn't showing properties.

"Sam," I said, "have you ever seen a millionaire real estate professional working out of a space like that?"

Long silence.

"No, I guess not," he said. "I guess not."

I explained to him that work environments count for or against our success—that they are reflections of our self-esteem and our self-image. Our surroundings at work need to be thoughtfully engineered to please us, please our workers, and delight our customers. Our surroundings make a statement to everybody, and we need to carefully decide what we want them to say.

What does old and funky say about your business, about you, and about your level of success?

What does crowded and too hot or too cold say to your workers about what you think of them?

What does your office say to an important visitor who is there to grace you with new business?

What does your basement cave say about you and how much good you can allow yourself to have?

THE FIX

Walk around your business quarters, inside and outside, basement to attic, with new eyes. Ask yourself as you stand and look, "What does my workspace say? What kind of mood does it create when I'm in it? When my people are in it? What kind of statement would I like it to make, and what would it take to have that happen—what specific changes would need to be made?"

Oh, but this could get expensive, your mind tells you.

Yes, but if you want to go to the numbers, don't forget to add up what it's already costing you in money and intangibles to leave it as is.

Your space may be a mixture of good and bad, assets and liabilities. Make a list of both. How could you strengthen your workspace assets and eliminate the liabilities? Decide what the priorities are and how much changing you would be willing to do.

Get feedback about this from someone you trust—someone who doesn't view this kind of thing exactly as you do. It should be someone who is successful and who has a professional space that you really like. Get some input and advice from that person before you decide what to do.

Your space matters to your success. A lot. When people love your workspace, it will affect your business for the better.

ASSETS	LIABILITIES
Everything is clean—everything. All the time.	There is a smudgy, cobwebby, or just plain dirty feel to things, a sense that the place needs a good deep cleaning.
Workstations are designed specifically for the work that is done there. A desk isn't a drafting table, and the top of a filing cabinet is not a computer stand.	One-size-fits-all, uncomfortable furniture is the norm, with not enough room. Work surfaces are not compatible with the work that is done on them—they are obstructed, too small, or too large, surfaces are too hard or soft.
Workspaces have reliable heating/cooling that is acceptable to most workers. Airflow is evenly and unnoticeably distributed.	You need to wear sweaters all winter and sweat in summer, and there are hot or cold areas around air vents. Drafty or steamy exterior doorways let too much of the outdoors in or too much of the indoors out.

ASSETS, CONT.	LIABILITIES, CONT.
Light! Well-lit public spaces are a must, as well as good light at each desk or work-station. Customizing light-ing to the needs of each area and to the work that is performed there is the ideal.	There's not enough light, too much light, or the wrong kind of light. You get ceiling light when you need a desk light, and there are areas that are too dark or too light. Too much light makes you flinch. Too little light, and you work in a cave.
Quiet—to think and create	External noise disrupts concentration, and studies show that it takes up to twenty minutes to regain lost concentration. That's a lot of lost productivity in a noisy place.
Paint, as well as all wall and ceiling coverings look fresh and clean, and colors are used everywhere to set the mood and support function.	You can see fading, crack-ing, discolored surfaces. Gray walls and carpeting aren't neutral—they're depressing.
Smells good and fresh in here!	You can smell funky, old-food, artificial, toxic, or unclean smells. There are inadequately ventilated public areas—kitchens, bathrooms, or storage areas. Bathroom air fresh-eners reek.

ASSETS, CONT.	LIABILITIES, CONT.
There's space to stand, space to move, stretch, and breathe! Space that's yours, not theirs.	Desks or cubes are too small or too close, leading to overcrowding of people, furniture, or equipment. Some areas aren't easy to access.
You have all the right equipment and supplies on hand that are needed for the work to be done.	You have outdated, inefficient equipment, outdated software or hardware, inadequate or low-quality supplies. (Cheap toilet paper says the wrong things about you.)

CHAPTER 25

I MATTER TO THIS COMPANY, TO MY TEAM, AND TO THE LARGER ORGANIZATION

To matter is to have importance and significance.

Mattering is not just connected to one's high stature or role in an organization, but also to the value of each person's unique presence and contribution. There is an operational baseline of what matters to a company in the sense that bodies must fill seats, and people must do acceptable work in each role at all levels in order for the business of the organization to succeed. This is the level of "performing the work" mattering, and indeed, the company needs that baseline of performance to function, so it is very important.

This is the level of contribution that most companies honor when they give recognition to someone for performance—that they do their job well or for a long time.

But mattering means much more than that. It is also about the person who does the work having importance beyond her position and the quality of her work. It means that she cares—that she is connected to others and contributes her work *and her personhood* in a meaningful way to her team, her company, and the larger work of the company. She is not a robot, and her personal being and abilities contribute in unique ways that add to her work competence and your good outcomes.

She has importance and significance in all these ways even if nobody rewards her for her contributions. There is some satisfaction just in her knowing this; the tree does indeed make a sound falling in the forest, even if nobody is there to hear it. She matters, even if nobody recognizes it.

But part of mattering at a more complete, happiness-producing level involves receiving recognition from others that confirms our significance and importance in this workplace. We need to see and hear recognition from others at work that we matter because it is good for our self-esteem maintenance, for our ability to put ourselves out there and take appropriate risks, and for our sense of loyalty to this place, its mission, and its people. It also helps us enjoy our work more and contribute to a happy, positive environment.

When we are children, we don't automatically know it when we are doing something great. We need our parents to tell us about it—to reflect our greatness back to us so we can know what it looks like and who we really are. This experience, repeated regularly over time, builds healthy self-esteem. Recognition is emotional nutrition, and the need for it doesn't go away as we get older. When your people know that they are important and that they have significance in these ways, it adds to their sense of well-being and calls forth more of their best efforts, more of their loyalty, and more of their happiness, all of which are contagious.

THE FIX

1. Say *"thank you"* often. Appreciate what others do well—in person or in a message, out loud or in a written note, when it happens or later.

2. Reward the person as well as performance. Someone's "can-do" attitude, someone else's great way with customers, another person's excellent communication skills.

3. Start meetings with appreciations—acknowledgments of the good things you are observing or hearing about an individual or team.

4. Give bonuses, gift cards, balloons, or a shopping spree at Walmart or Costco.

5. Get your other leaders and supervisors together to brainstorm meaningful forms of recognition so you are always ready to sufficiently recognize the good that people do.

ASSETS	LIABILITIES
You look for and show your appreciation for the things that your people do right.	You look for problems to fix and point out shortcomings wherever you see them.

ASSETS, CONT.	LIABILITIES, CONT.
You give your people rewards of real value beyond their paychecks for a job well done.	There are punishments for mistakes but no rewards for excellence.
You acknowledge personal excellence as well as job performance—honesty, reliability, length of service, good communication, and working well with others.	There is only recognition for work performance and achievement of work goals.
You lay out for your workers how their contributions have specific positive impacts beyond their position and their departments—how they are connected to and affect the organization as a whole for the better.	Workers in areas or departments work in their own ecosystems with little connection or reference to the bigger picture of the company-as-a-whole.
You go the extra mile whenever possible to be there for your workers when they need extra support for something job or home related, including such things as more project support or materials and time away for illness or personal leave.	You rely on policies when workers request extra support for their job or their personal well-being. If there's not a policy for it, it doesn't happen.

CHAPTER 26

I AM PROUD OF MY ORGANIZATION

When I am proud of my organization, it means I think it is doing a lot of things right.

Those things might include: what the business of the organization is or how it's done; great company values; how the leaders treat people; the achievements of the company; the high quality of the people who work there; leadership style, vision, or mission, or the way they give back to their community; exciting plans for the future; support for a good cause; the generosity of leadership toward those who work for them; their policies of inclusion; their commitment to great customer service; their honesty and integrity; the sense of family in the workforce; leaders' openness to feedback; worker-friendly policies; progressive and creative management practices; and the fresh cookies every Friday.

Come to think of it, that's a pretty good ingredient list for company pride that you can use to create more pride and happiness at work—and also happiness for everyone who touches the company.

THE FIX

Start some conversations: What are you proud of about your company? What are your people proud of? What do your customers like most about your company—why do they like it, and why are they loyal? Use meetings, personal conversations, and surveys to communicate about this.

Find out: What could the company do more of that people would be proud of? Invite ideas from everyone and reward the ones you want to encourage. This process should be transparent so everyone is in on it. Communicate results and reactions, and let everyone know when you put an idea into action. Enlist everybody in some part of the implementation.

Start something good: Capture the answers to the above questions and launch a company pride initiative based on the best ideas. Communicate results and feedback, let everyone know when you put each part of the initiative into action, and get people involved in the rollout.

ASSETS	LIABILITIES
Define and encourage company pride with your people. Do this "out loud" so everyone can participate.	Don't start this conversation because your workers might not be proud of your company, and that would be embarrassing.
Encourage workers to name what they do for the company that they are proud of. Share this information widely.	You decide, without worker input, what your company is proud of and put it in your advertising.
Acknowledge and reward the people in your organization who are exemplary—those who stand out for their contributions to company spirit and stature. Do this on a regular basis.	The business of the company is to make money, and if that's happening, don't rock the boat with all this other stuff.

CHAPTER 27

HOW TO ROLL OUT HAPPINESS IN YOUR WORKPLACE, BASED ON THIS BOOK

First, start with the scores and strategies you wrote down in the "Give yourself a score…" and "Take action for traction" sections at the end of every topic in this book. If you haven't had a chance to fill in those sections, now is the time, before you forget.

I put those in the book so you can assess how you are doing with each topic and quickly figure out some things you can do to improve your happiness in any area that needs it. There is gold in your collected answers. Gathered together as a list, those scores and strategies will make up your own highly effective plan to increase your happiness at work. If you really do this—make the list and then start working on each item one after the other—you will transform your work life for the better and claim happiness in ways you couldn't before. You will also transform your leadership and your relationships with your people, which will allow them to grow, flourish, and live up to their potential.

1. *You must start with a basically functional, fair workplace* if you want to increase the happiness of the people who work for you. If you have an unhappy workplace where people don't get along and are habitually at odds with each other, or if your people have grievances about the work itself—about how they are treated or paid, or about working conditions and supervision—these things must be corrected.

   If these situations persist unchecked, your efforts to introduce more happiness into your workplace will probably fail. There must be a foundation of some level of basic worker satisfaction already in place in order for the steps in this book to take hold and bear fruit.

Here's the next step, the best step of all, when you think your people are ready for it:

2. *Design a "Workplace Happiness" initiative,* starting from some of the "Fix" sections in this book. Those sections are meant to focus tightly on realistic, effective things you can do in your organization to bring about more happiness for you and your workers. You might want to set up an initiative project team that you would charge with designing it. It's good to have a planner or project manager on this team, and it would probably be a good idea for you to personally monitor its progress closely to be sure the initiative design stays on track. Once the design part is done, work together to time the implementation of the various

elements of it by making a rollout plan that is SMART: *Specific, Measurable, Achievable, Realistic, and Time-lined.*

3. *Be aware that people resist change.* Even positive change stirs up resistance. The roots of this reaction go all the way back to the beginning of our species. It is an unbreakable rule passed down in our genes and our old, lingering lizard brain that we should never deviate from the known path where there are no tigers. Exploring new paths used to increase our odds of becoming a meal for a tiger, so resisting change is a deeply instinctual survival reaction. It doesn't matter whether or not the change is good, the reaction will still happen, so be prepared for it. Don't think you've failed and don't stop your efforts when it happens—just hold steady, find new ways to stay on message, and be persistent.

Some ways to introduce change effectively are:

1. *Introduce changes to your people in small pieces and slowly.* This means you should have a plan for a slow, step-by-step rollout of your Workplace Happiness Initiative (or whatever you decide to call it). You will incite a lot of resistance if you make a big deal out of this and roll it all out at once with your version of trumpets and ticker tape. People react to change best when it is taken in small bites, with time in between to digest each bite. A slow rollout is good for you and your initiative team, too, because it gives time for feedback so you can make adjustments to the plan as needed along the way.

2. *Involve your formal and informal leaders in this change initiative.* Informal leaders are those people in the ranks to whom

other workers look for guidance and direction. Members of your design team should be brought up to speed well ahead of time, too, so they are familiar and comfortable with what they're doing pre-rollout. Be sure they are all really on board so they can create buzz about the initiative before it is pushed out to everyone else.

3. *Explain your initiative widely within your company, and explain it well, in every available way.* Give people the facts about how much better happy companies are and what the real benefits are. Tell them about The Eight Things Workers Want the Most and let them know you are committed to their having each and every one. Let them know that you are personally making changes, too, so you can be happy and better support happiness in your workplace.

4. There's an old saying in the business training world: tell them what you are going to tell them, tell them the thing itself, then tell them what you told them, and include a call to action. This is a good template for how to communicate your changes to your people. Broadcast what you are doing so people don't have to guess. Use every means you've got—at meetings, in the newsletter, on social media. Here's why great communication at this stage is so important: people will be anxious about change, and if they don't know what's going on, *they will make it up,* and what they make up will always be negative and fearful and will spread like wildfire. Always keep your people in the loop about changes.

5. *Once your happiness initiative is out there, don't let it fade away.* When you're trying to make a big change like this, it amounts to changing your company culture. Company culture is "the way we

do things and how we treat people around here." Creating a context for a happy company certainly will have a lot of impacts on your culture, most of them good and some of them unintended. Therefore, you ought not just throw it all out there and then let it sink or swim. There are people who, for whatever reasons, are comfortable with the culture you had, so you need to protect your initiative and deal effectively with overt or covert resistance.

It would be good to design your initiative to include some systematic monitoring and collecting of post-initiative outcomes as well as some general tracking of whether happiness does indeed increase for you and your people, both short and long term. Good results should be shouted from the rooftops. It will be very important to your people, once they buy in, that you keep this going and remain visibly committed to it. Any halfheartedness or neglect will damage or kill the initiative. Keep it going. Get your people to help you keep it going. Measure the outcomes and publish them. Old habits of mood and behavior are hard to break, so your collective care and attention are needed to help happiness find a lasting home in your workplace.

A word of warning: if you start this initiative and give people a taste of something new and better and then allow it to fall flat, you will have disrupted your previous culture with nothing better to take its place, and your people won't be comfortable going back. You will leave them in cultural limbo, and nothing good will come of that.

And lastly, we at Happy Workplace Consulting Group stand ready to help with your happiness enhancement effort in any way we can. We have good people and great tools to assist you, and we are always just an email, a text, a phone call, or a videoconference call away. We'd be happy to consult with you initially at no charge, too. You may contact us as follows:

HAPPY WORKPLACE
C O N S U L T I N G G R O U P

"A happy workplace inspires people to do their best work, which makes the companies that employ them exceptionally profitable and stable.

At Happy Workplace Consulting Group we join with company leaders to build happiness-based success into their organizations at all levels, as a culture and a practice."

Doug Hickok, President
Phone: 410-280-1400
Email: doug@myhappyworkplace.com
Website: www.myhappyworkplace.com

DOUG HICKOK is the President of *Happy Workplace Consulting Group.* He has more than twenty years of experience as an executive coach and communication expert specializing in leadership development.

Doug is a Certified Imago Educator (psychology and communication) and a nationally known author, trainer, and speaker. In addition to writing this book, he is also the author of *How to Succeed with Your Great Business Idea.*

Doug has taught in the Executive Education program at the Management Institute of the Robins School of Business, University of Richmond, in Richmond, Virginia. He is also an executive coach for The Honor Foundation, an organization that prepares Navy Seals for their transitions from the military into civilian business life.

Doug Hickok is a member of the International Association of Coaching, the Association for Talent Development, and the Academy of Management.

He lives with his wife Betsy in Annapolis, Maryland.

....

THE BEST WAY TO STAND OUT OVER THE COMPETITION

Which physician makes more money, the general practitioner or the heart specialist?

It's the heart specialist, of course.

There is a similar perception of greater value that operates in business. People trust and pay more for an expert in a field who has a well-defined, singular focus. A business that does not have this single-focus expertise won't attract customers as well as one that does.

What kind of focus am I talking about? You need to be an expert in one thing and be known for just that one thing.

Nike did so well with this approach that they are still known primarily for their athletic shoes. Even though the Nike brand now produces a variety of other athletic clothing, their diverse products are still grouped around their single core focus—shoes.

You can sell other services and products as long as they support your single focus of expertise.

When I started my business years ago, I enjoyed doing both business coaching and skills training for companies and conferences, so I billed myself as an "executive coach and trainer." Try as I might, my business sputtered until I followed the advice of a wise friend and chose just one thing as the focus of my expertise—executive coaching. Business picked up steadily, and instead of falling off because of my focus on just that one area, the training side increased dramatically, too!

I found out that if you are known and trusted as an expert in your specialty, customers will also engage you to do the other things you do because they come to trust you, and they become willing to try your other offerings, too.

Lawyers are good at a single focus.

If you go to a law firm's website, you'll find all the lawyers listed there, each with a specialty beside his or her name. Notice that there is usually only one specialty per person. People have more confidence in someone who is an expert at one thing because they presume that the person knows just about everything there is to know about that thing.

So, if you are going to open a computer services store, what specific part of computer services will be your specialty? If you are going to be a marketing consultant, what specific kind of marketing will be your specialty? If you're going to sell clothing, what specific type of clothing will you sell—clothing about which you are an expert?

One of my very favorite breakfast restaurants sells just about every type of breakfast food you can imagine. What they are famous for, though, is their huge Dutch apple pancakes. They are experts at Dutch apple pancakes, *and* they do a booming business in all those other breakfast dishes, too.

You want to become known as an expert in something and make that something the focus of your brand, the centerpiece of all your marketing.

Be aware that anytime you use the word "and" when you describe what you do, you have wandered away from your specialty focus.

I remember seeing a cartoon once with an image of a tired old guy leaning on the sill of a service window, waiting for a customer, all by himself in a hut beside the road.

The sign over his head read:
Fred's Fill Dirt & Croissants

You really don't want to be that guy.

www.ingramcontent.com/pod-product-compliance
Lightning Source LLC
Chambersburg PA
CBHW060843280326
41934CB00007B/905